I0707124

Tales from an American Childhood: Recollection & Revelation

Dr. John C. Thomas, Ph.D.

DEDICATION

I dedicate this book to all my former and current teachers, formal and informal. I owe a special debt of gratitude, however, to my High School English teacher, Ladonna Koledin for introducing me to so many great writers and pushing me to improve my own writing. Whatever future America is to have, it will depend heavily on the quality of our teachers.

CONTENTS

ACKNOWLEDGMENTS

I'd like to thank readers of earlier drafts of this book as well as commentators on earlier drafts of some of the chapters, many of which were originally presented in my blog, https://petersironwood.wordpress.com. I'd especially like to thank my wife Wendy Kellogg for her thoughtful comments and her reminders that the reader is not actually in my head and needs words written on the page to follow my many leaps from point A to point J.

1 AFTER THE FALL

Only a few scattered memories from my pre-literate era waft around in my head. Like swirling autumn leaves, early memories shine brightly with vivid hues but can only be caught randomly, often at some distance from the tree of their origin and context. I recall staring at swelling giant green ocean waves over the railing of a skyscraper-tall ship. I see the image clearly still because I grabbed and held on to that memory for my collection. That image, however, lacks attachment to the origin or destination of that trans-Atlantic voyage.

The shiny red toy gun flashes in my inner eye, but no stem attaches to a giver or an occasion.

I can re-hear my father's quavery voice, as he hunkers down in the bow of the paddle boat, cautioning us to do the same because of the airplanes overhead. But it holds no connection to his time in the army or the knee to ankle shiny blackened shrapnel wound where his left shin was supposed to be.

Once my formal schooling began though, whether because of maturity or training, my memories began to cluster and connect to a framework. Whether this makes my later memories more accurate or less accurate I cannot say, but that they are different — this is not in doubt.

In the first grade, we began to learn to print. I actually already knew how to print. I had taught myself before school began. I suppose that was part of the problem. Even now, I don't make my letters and numbers with the same "strokes" that most people do. Anyway, we were supposed to be learning to print, and since I was there, I wanted to play the game along with everyone else. I had no desire to be "difficult" or "create a spectacle."

With our giant awkward green pencils poised above our cheap, lined, gray-yellow paper, we were to copy our teacher's printing. At that point, blackboards were still black and chalk was still white. Miss Wilkins had neatly printed: "TODAY IS TUESDAY. TODAY IS TUESDAY. TODAY IS TUESDAY." We were to fill our paper with this vital all-caps phrase. Indeed, it *was* Tuesday, but I really only needed to print it once to remember that. In fact, zero times would have sufficed. But, you see, there were *rules* in schools. There were rules at home as well, but by comparison, very few. Home rules almost always made some modicum of sense, even to a six year old. School rules seemed part of some elaborate, quasi-religious, magical ritual or militaristic game imposed without explanation or exception.

This surprised me only a little because home and school *smelled* quite different. The black slate board had a smell, dark and clean and sharp. The chalk had a smell, that was attractive but choking. The cheap shiny paper had it's own cheap shiny smell. And, if you took the time to notice (which most kids did), the bare wood of the giant green pencils smelled quite nice and much better than the shiny green paint part of the pencil. In fact, volunteering to sharpen pencils was a job most of us were eager for, not only for that wonderful woody odor but also for the idea that we were making our own tools, and possibly our own weapons. We also got to make these really cool papery shreds of pencil wood. Apart from all that, we learned a skill. Cranking the handle of the sharpener had to be done with a certain fluidity. Meanwhile, you had to be careful to keep the pencil horizontal or you could break the emerging point. The primitive machine kept trying to grab the pencil and whirl it around. It much preferred that to sharpening. But my job was to keep that pencil firm and do it all with grace and rhythm so that a perfect point emerged. We were forbidden even to whisper in class and could only speak when called upon. But pencil sharpening! That was another matter entirely. We filled the air with noise! We weren't supposed to yell or shout in class, but we could raise a real ruckus with the grinding of the wood. When sharpening a pencil, I could feel the blood rush into my arms and feel the pulsing muscles. This was one of the few times, outside of recess, when I felt *alive* in school.

By contrast, filling lines of paper with the same phrase over and over held no such attractions. I understood the task at hand. I needed to fill up the page with "TODAY

IS TUESDAY." And, so I began. First I made a long vertical line for the "T" letters. Then I crossed every "T." Then, I made a long vertical column of "O's" and another long vertical line for the "D's." I began to add the bows for the "D's." Just as I was about halfway done with my "D-bows" however, the teacher yanked me out of my chair. She screamed (did I mention that we pupils were not allowed to yell?) as she marched me out into the hallway. Then, she grabbed me by my shoulders and shook me. As she screamed, she began to sob. I felt kind of bad for her, but I honestly had no idea what she was so upset about.

Sadly, this was not my only run-in with my first grade teacher. We also had a spirited debate about whether heavier objects fell faster than lighter objects. She seemed quite satisfied that her example of the rock and the feather should leave any sane person convinced, but whether sane or not, it didn't convince *me*. My father and grandfather were both engineers and my grandfather subscribed to Sky and Telescope, Scientific American, and The Atlantic Monthly. I probably perused the pictures more than the text, but I also read articles from a very early age. Whether from reading or from talking with Dad and Grandpa, I somehow had heard about Galileo's little experiment performed from the Leaning Tower of Pisa. I explained this to her as best I could, but she refused to believe it. Again, she gave the example of the stone and the feather. She must have thought me more than a bit dense.

Perhaps that is why she thought so little of it one bright summery day when one of my classmates pushed me down the concrete steps in front of our school door. Such a head over heels tumble presented the oddest sensations! I recall being astounded by the seemingly random jumble of images swirling by. My head didn't feel too great either, but I think the sudden lack of control over what I was seeing and doing was even more terrifying. Typically, one of the few school rules that did make sense to me was that we were not allowed to hit, kick, bite or shove other kids. I've never felt much inclined to injure others so I didn't mind following this rule at all. But here I was, not having been punched or kicked, but victim of a potentially far more dangerous rule violation. At the time, I didn't think of it so much as dangerous as it was rude. And, beyond that, it clearly constituted an egregious violation of the rules. If we were going to have all these school rules, why should they not apply to everyone? Why should someone get away with pushing me down the concrete steps when I had seen the mildest of pushes and punches get punished enthusiastically?

At the time, I could generate no coherent explanation. The cognitive confusion about how adults failed to meet my expectations simply added to my perceptual confusion from free-fall tumbling. It seemed as though the world were saying to me, "All Bets are Off" and "Adult Authorities Cannot be Trusted" and "You never know."

Who *could* be trusted, then? Well, my beautiful dog Mel (rhymes with "meal") for one. My Dad brought Mel back from Portugal. Mel was a beautiful honey-colored Cocker Spaniel. Mel and I loved each other unconditionally. A few weeks earlier, however, I had heard my parents talking about giving him away because other kids in the neighborhood were teasing him and Mel, tied up, was snapping at them. He had a wire lead connected at one end to his collar and the other end was looped around a horizontal wire. Some kids quickly saw just how far he could go and found great pleasure in getting him to run to the end of his lead and then watch his neck snap back as he reached the end. This infuriated Mel and he snarled and snapped at them. My folks were worried that a bite could lead to a lawsuit.

I made them promise not to sell Mel. And, they didn't. When I got home from school one day, Mel was gone. But he hadn't been sold at all. Not at all. He had been "put to sleep." Our small two bedroom bungalow had one main hall closet with a blue quilt folded up at the back. That's where I went to hang out for the next few hours. I didn't much want to talk to my parents. Not about Mel. Not about anything. It seemed to me, that if anyone should have been "put to sleep" it would have been the kids who were teasing him. I just sat in the dark on the cool blue quilt crying for Mel.

Despite what my first grade teacher might think, sometimes small, light things — things even so light as a soul — can fall very fast, very fast indeed.

2 INVENTING A NEW COLOR

After Dad returned from World War II, he married my mom and nine months later, I was born. In my earliest years, we lived in a number of places near Akron, Ohio, and when I was about three and a half years old, we moved to Portugal. My dad headed up a tire factory there. I don't remember much about Portugal, but I do recall going with him to some of his fancy dinners. For reasons I did not understand at the time, when I was five, my mother and I took the long ocean liner ride back to America without my dad. Mom and I lived with Grandpa and Grandma at their house. I attended a kindergarten in Firestone Park and had a very nice teacher. I loved kindergarten.

I missed my dad but liked Grandpa and Grandma. She told me "Old Pete" stories and we listened to radio shows such as *Roy Rogers, Hop-along Cassidy*, and *Tom Corbett and the Space Cadets*. "Little Grandma" lived there too. She was my grandpa's mom and stood quite stooped over; she was very tiny, very old, and looked exactly like an old wrinkled Native American. Much later, I learned that that was because she was Native American or perhaps half Native American. I loved "Little Grandma."

Grandpa worked as an engineer and designed airplane wings, among other things. Grandpa was also a painter and his beautiful and detailed oils hung in large wooden frames throughout his house. Mostly, these were landscapes but there were also portraits and my personal favorite depicted two warships firing cannons at each other while being tossed on giant whitecaps. Grandpa taught me many things. Naturally, I wanted to return the favor. When I was about five, I overheard him saying that it was impossible to invent a new color. Well, I could definitely teach him something about that! I loved the idea of being an inventor.

In the middle of kindergarten, my dad returned from Portugal and re-united with my mom. He bought a house and we moved away to a different neighborhood. I had to start school in a new kindergarten populated by complete strangers. The very first day, my new teacher decided that I would lead the parade and draped the rope of a large bass drum around my neck. I didn't want to play the drum and I didn't want anything draped around my neck. As the new kid in class, I definitely did not want to be singled out as the leader of the band. I made that about as clear as I could to her, but nonetheless, I ended up marching around the room with the heavy drum around my neck. I hated kindergarten.

My dad worked as an engineer and my mom was a teacher so both of them were gone all day. They hired a housekeeper to take care of me. And, somehow, after the first day, I convinced our housekeeper that I did not need to go to kindergarten any more. This was fine with her and more than fine with me because she was nice enough to give me my favorite lunch every day — a jar of maraschino cherries! They were so sweet and such a vibrant vivid red. And, not only were the cherries themselves delicious. The jars proved to be perfect for my experiments! So, in the second half of kindergarten, I did not play "Grocery Store" or "Postman" or lead any more parades. I stayed home instead and spent my time inventing a new color to show Grandpa. I had a paint set and I had water and I had lots of empty maraschino cherry jars. It was all a matter of time and careful work. At last, *I* would be able to teach *Grandpa* something. I love teaching.

After many weeks of careful work, I finally created a new color. When grandpa and grandma came to visit, I was ready. Under my bed were about 40 teeny jars of diluted paint. Thirty-nine of them were merely failed attempts. But one of them contained the prize! I carefully crawled under the bed and located my invention, slid it out, and scampered into the living room where the adults practiced their buzz-talk. Buzz-talk sounded serious and low but didn't actually mean anything so far as I could tell. Surely, no-one could mind if I interrupted buzz-talk by announcing my invention. I proudly held out my prize to grandpa. Grandpa was very smart, so the fact that he did not immediately catch the significance of this jar surprised me. He merely glanced at the watery liquid in the maraschino cherry jar without comment. I'd better clue him in, I thought. "Grandpa! It's a new color!" He glanced at it again and said, "I've seen it before." And just like that, he went back to buzz-talk! Crest-fallen, I wandered back to my bedroom and placed the prize beneath my bed with all the failed experiments. Apparently, this was just another one. Despite this terrible turn of events, I hardly gave up. I just redoubled my efforts. I knew there was a new color out there somewhere and I would find the perfect mix and next time be successful! I loved the challenge.

Grandpa had already taught me that red and yellow paint make orange; that yellow and blue paint make green; and that red and blue paint make purple. So, obviously, most of my experiments involved various proportions of red and green, purple and yellow or orange and blue. Most of these recipes ended up as fairly similar shades of gray-brown. But if I mixed very carefully, I produced not dull gray-brown but something with a slight tinge of something…new! I somehow found other jars because I needed more than just the supply offered by one a day lunch-time maraschino cherry jars. I didn't think bigger jars would have anything to do with inventing a new color, but it was possible. After a few weeks, grandpa and grandma came over to visit again. And again, I interrupted their dull living room buzz talk by showing off my latest creation. This time, I was more apprehensive. The first time, after all, I had known for *sure* I had a new color. This time, I was uncertain. I waited for the right opportunity — that slight pause in the buzz-talk — to display my new creation.

"I've seen that," Grandpa said and turned back to buzz-talk. I wasn't yet old enough to argue. And, even now, years later, if someone claims they have seen a color and you think they have not seen the color, I am still not sure how to argue. Convincing other people is seldom an easy task and convincing them that their own perception is limited — that is extremely difficult. Many times, I have heard the old saw, "In the land of the blind, the one-eyed man is king." I actually doubt that. I suspect in the land of the blind, the one-eyed man is more likely to be declared in league with Satan and end up being stoned to death.

Let's think about this. Suppose you possess the one functioning eye in the land of the blind. Say everyone is hungry and you see a berry bush a couple hundred yards away. Now what? Well, you could say, "Hey, everyone! I see a berry bush over there (uselessly pointing). Let's go pick some berries." Everyone else says, "What berry bush? I don't feel one. I don't hear one. I don't smell one. There's no berry bush. Be quiet and stop talking nonsense." Alternatively, you could just quietly walk over to the berry bush and bring back a small quantity for everyone to share. Of course, if everyone went, you could bring back a lot more, but no-one wants to follow you. You bring back some berries but people would be suspicious. They might well think you had been hiding these and had many more you failed to share.

Similarly, if you saw a pack of hyenas headed your way and warned people, the blind might well think you were in league with the hyenas. After all, you were the first one to know about them. They think you must have *told* the hyenas where everyone was. At long last, if you were the one-eyed person, you might be pretty tempted to put out that other eye. Life would run a lot smoother for you.

Alternatively, you could leave the tribe and live on your own. And, many people do make this choice, essentially. But it's a pretty lonely life. You could try to patiently explain that just as sometimes they could smell things they could not feel and feel things they could not smell, and hear things they could not yet feel or smell, that you could "see"…ah, that's the sticky bit. How do you explain sight to the unsighted?

Of course, my grandfather was not blind. Far from it. He was not only an adult, with more power and experience and knowledge than a five year old kid; he was, in fact, an *artist*. He was an *expert* on color. I could see evidence of his expertise everywhere. His paintings adorned both our houses. So, he probably was right about the particular colors I had shown him so far. But that didn't mean that I couldn't invent one next time that was truly new. So, back to the lab, I went. I failed a few more times and eventually gave up. Inventing a new color really was impossible.

Or was it?

Many years later, I attended an art exhibit in Pittsburgh. It featured many kinds of "modern art" including a very cool kinesthetic art exhibit. In one exhibit, I simply stood on a platform in front of a large rotating disk. I watched the disk rotate wondering what the point of this mundane wheel was — until quite unexpectedly, the disk stilled itself and *I* was rotating in the other direction! Of particular interest were some extremely large extremely brightly colored canvasses which featured huge swaths of complementary colors. If I stared for a good long time at the super bright red and then moved my eyes over to the super bright green, the combination of temporal and spatial contrast produced an unearthly bright green, a "supersaturated" color impossible to produce by merely using one pigment. While I had not personally invented this, at least I now had experienced a color it was likely my grandpa never had. I could not really check this out though because he was long dead. Of course, I have met him in dreams many times and in the dreams he's not really dead. It was all a big mistake. In my dreams, supersaturated colors paint landscapes that even Grandpa has to admit are new colors. I love the thought that even the wisdom of elders may be fallible and changes over time.

My grandpa knew that humans are all mortal, of course, but he was also cognizant of humanity's legacy of fragmentary art, some of which was thousands of years old. Perhaps he thought that art provides a kind of immortality. When I was about ten, grandpa visited Europe and saw many of the oil paintings of the "Old Masters" that he greatly admired. He saw with his own eyes that, over time, the oil that they had originally used had turned yellowish. Father Time himself had invented new (and duller) colors for these artists. When Grandpa returned from Europe, he switched from oil painting to water colors. Beyond that, he limited himself to using only three pigments, all of which were oxides of metals. He was also very careful in his choice of canvases. He stuck to these constraints so that *his* paintings, unlike those of the "Old Masters," would not yellow or fade with time.

Grandpa's paintings were designed by an artist/engineer to be stable and unchanging over time. When Grandpa died, I inherited quite a few of my favorite water colors and I can testify that the colors were extremely stable over time. They remained stable, that is, up until the time we moved to California and almost everything we owned burned up in a moving van fire. What was burned up included all our furniture, electronics, papers, and almost all clothing, and grandpa's paintings. All the carefully laid pigments of metals were altered forever. All of the work and effort were now white ash floating somewhere in the sky near Continental Divide, New Mexico. A little carelessness on the part of a trucker in too much of a hurry, perhaps, to check the wheel bearing lubrication and the whole truck went up in flames. Robert Burns' ("…the best laid plans of mice and men…") comes to mind.

It seems to me that *America* once comprised a long-standing collaborative work of art involving many artists and many colors. She was a painting of scale and magnificence, though never completed. Every shade of the rainbow and more besides swept from sea to shining sea. The painting combined portraiture and landscape, scenes of war and peace, city, country, rivers, lakes, deep woods, and shining plains. Yet, somehow, people became impatient with the progress of the painting. Maybe, they thought, the work would go faster if we just painted the whole canvas white. They no longer cared what the end result looked like. They just wanted to get done so we could move on to the next project. We really couldn't take the time to make sure the bearings were lubricated. And, now, the transport has burned up along with the painting. What's left? Scattered white flakes of ash snowing down on the countryside.

I love irony, but I loved the paintings more.

At some point, grandpa said something else to me about color. He said that most people look at color in the light but that there is also color in the shadow. And, so, despite the deepening, darkening shadows, I am trying to see the color hidden there in those shadows. It is too soon to know whether I am inventing a new color, inventing a new way to look at color, or just seeing what is actually an after-image, beautiful for now, but certain to soon fade to the dull white gray of old and sooted snow. Maybe one of us can invent a new color or a new way of painting or a new way of looking or a new way of helping people be less impatient with the slow careful progress required for a timeless, collaborative work of art. Inventing new colors is not easy work; that I can say for sure, nor is it trivial to restore a rainbow of true color once the color has faded to a uniform and pasty gray.

Perhaps I'll buy a jar of maraschino cherries.

A bunch of us first-graders were waiting to take our turns in some kind of race. While we waited on the edge of the playground for our name to be called, I looked at and then *through* the hurricane fence in front of us. I discovered that I could look through the fence and see another fence. This second fence was gigantic and far away. Yet, it was also quite close! Indeed, it seemed as though this was no ordinary fence, but a *magic* fence that I could place where I liked just by changing something in my head. I tried to share this information about the magic fence with the other kids waiting with me but I failed to get them to see the magic fence. I didn't have long. It was my turn to race.

And race I did — but rather badly. I was amazed to discover that I was *not* the fastest runner in first grade. It had always seemed to me that I ran extremely fast! That's how I felt inside. But many kids in my class ran faster than I did. Even many girls ran faster than I did which seemed at the time absolutely impossible. How could I feel so fast running and yet be slower than so many other kids? Even the fattest kid in the class ran faster!

Later in first grade, upon returning from a ten day stint at the hospital for pneumonia, my parents bought me bunk beds and covered the bunk beds with a green bedspread which had a repeating pattern of identical and quite stylized white flowers. I could lay on the bedspread, look at the pattern and then look *through* the bedspread to another larger bedspread father away. In fact, I could find

several bedspreads at various distances. I experimented
by getting closer or father away from the bedspread and
by fooling with my eyes. I did not understand exactly
what was happening, but one thing was clear. The world
that I had thought was "out there" proved very
changeable under my own actions and volitions. I could
"change" the world out there — or at least how it
appeared — *by what I did in my own head.*

My grandmother supervised the Sunday School at the
Methodist church my family attended. Sunday School
seemed super neat. For instance, I memorized the most
verses from the Bible of anyone in my class and as a
reward, won a glow-in-the-dark cross. I was supposed to
look at this at night and derive comfort from it. I don't
recall that working but what I *did* discover, which was
really cool was this: if I put my eye right up to that cross
in total darkness, I could see tiny flashes of light. The
cross, like so many "glow in the dark" items back then,
included both phosphorescent paint and radium laced
paint. Same with my "glow in the dark" watch. When the
lights first went out, these items would glow quite
brightly from the phosphorescence. But even hours later,
when that effect had completely vanished, there was still
a faint glow from the radium paint. When placed directly
on the eye, however, there was an effect like beholding a
blurry bout of heat lightning.

Our Sunday School teacher told us that when we prayed,
we went to heaven! That certainly seemed kind of cool. I
wasn't *exactly* sure what heaven was like, but in at least
some of the pictures, there were some beautiful angels
and it would certainly be fun to meet *them;* especially the

one who looked exactly like Mary Ellen Liptack, a beautiful dark-eyed beauty in my class. So, I decided to test out our Sunday School's promise. I sat in the pews, closed my eyes, and prayed just as sincerely as I possibly could. When I was praying up a storm, I suddenly snapped open my eyes! And there I was! In Sunday School. I hadn't even moved to a different seat. No clouds. No heaven. And worst of all, no angels, not even Mary Ellen.

I tried it again. Same result. I wondered whether opening my eyes could somehow *instantly* bring me back from heaven to Akron, Ohio. That seemed unlikely. But I tried a few experiments in which I would pray hard and then not open my eyes, but just notice whether I still felt the hard wooden pew, and smelled the same musty curtain smell and hear the same kids breathing and fidgeting around me. Well, in case you are wondering, it didn't matter which sense or senses I used, I never got the slightest hint that I had gone to heaven. It not only didn't look like heaven; it didn't sound like it, smell like it or feel like it either. This was disappointing because one of the angels pictured in my "Red Letter Testament" Bible Study book (the Mary Ellen Liptack angel) looked out of that book right at me! Her beautiful eyes seemed to invite me to join her in heaven. But how? I don't think I had quite figured out that this was an "artist's conception" of what a beautiful angel might look like (e.g., a girl and just my age!). No, I knew she was *there* and I wanted to meet her.

About this time, I began to notice that my grandfather never joined us at Church. This seemed odd. At last I asked about it and he said he didn't go because he didn't believe in God! What? This seemed pretty inconceivable to me because *everyone* else around me kept talking about God as though He were real and definite. The way people talked gave not the slightest hint that God was something only *some* people believed in. God was portrayed as definitely *there.* There were paintings of God, for instance. Some of the illustrations in my books looked almost photographic in their realism. It made no sense that people would treat God as real if He were not.

My next door neighbor on Johnson Street played all sorts of games with me. I don't recall her name; she was a cute freckled red-head though occasionally, she was quite mean. She liked to tie up people or put tape over their mouths. But I really didn't have that many choices of people to play with. One day, on the way to Sunday School, my parents and I chanced to meet her and *her* parents. We were all dressed, as they say, in our "Sunday finest." So, I did the polite thing and greeted her warmly, "Hello, little S*** A**." All at once *everyone's faces* including the little girl's exploded into *horrified expressions.* I just used one of the main greetings that she used. I had no idea what the phrase meant or even the individual words. Later, after I was punished, I still persisted to try to find out how these words could possibly have so much power. My parents couldn't even bring themselves to tell me. My mother delegated this task to my grandfather. Perhaps looking back on it, his being an atheist meant he could say words like this or at least explain them.

He took me with him into the landing area in the stairway to the basement. Grandpa's house had some of the coolest features including a "Root Cellar", a "Coal Cellar" and a "Disappearing Stairway." In addition, Grandpa had a rock garden, a vegetable garden, a staircase and the house itself had *three* doors. There was a front door into a small entry off the living room. The back door went directly into the kitchen from a passageway near the garage. And, there was a third door that led off the basement stairs onto the patio near the apple tree that my mom had planted as a kid. My grandfather kept that door locked and no-one was allowed to use it. And that seemed a shame because *our* house only had *two* doors. It seemed to me, if you had a house with *three* doors, you would want to use all three! Anyway, it was near that door as he was emptying some trash that he explained what those magic words referred to.

He did *not* explain why they were powerful. He did *not* explain why my companion acted shocked when I used the very words I had learned from her and she *often* referred to me and other playmates with this phrase. He did *not* explain why *everyone* had been upset. Once he explained what it referred to, I could kind of understand why *she* might not want to be called that although that was what she called everyone else. But why had her parents been so upset and why had my parents been so upset? It was one of those "explanations" that only explained the surface of a complex tangle of issues.

With a longer perspective, I can say that *most* so-called explanations fall short. They tell you why someone picked a particular color to paint their car. They don't explain how cars work or why we have so many cars in America and such limited public transportation. When it comes to religion, most explanations seem very much about the color of the paint. It's very hard to dig beneath that to find out how people really *relate* to their religion. And, this too always struck me as odd, especially for people who claim that their religion is a central part of who they are. Perhaps, it is not so much that people are *unwilling* to explain how religion works for them as they are *unable* to explain it.

After all, I altered my perception of the hurricane fence and the repeating pattern bedspread long before I understood how I managed. In fact, as a kid, I never found anyone else who either could or wanted to use this technique. In college, I read a book (I think by John Dewey or Donald O. Hebb but I'm not sure) and discovered that this author had also learned this same trick at an early age. Indeed, I still find it a useful skill many years later. For example, if I am bored sitting somewhere across from people at a table, I can "merge" the images of their heads to make a composite image. That's kind of fun. In grad school, before "Compare" functions, I found it useful to compare hexadecimal disk dumps by putting them side by side and crossing my eyes until the two dumps overlapped character by character. Anything that differed between the disk dumps popped out instantly. While I thought it might be a useful skill for others and explained how to do it when asked, I never felt the slightest urge to make *everyone* learn this skill. I never claimed it was the *only* way to look at the world or even the *best* way to look at the world.

I never seemed to get into an argument with people about forming clear double images. If I decided to see two apples — one image with each eye — instead of converging my views to see one image, it never seemed much of a big deal to me or to anyone else. If I said, "It looks to me right now like there are two apples" and someone said, "Yes, but there is really only one" then I would just say, "Yeah, I know. But it's kind of fun to see double sometimes." If they didn't feel like doing that, why would that bother me?

Of course, one could argue that seeing double is just a private exercise but that religion comes into play when it comes to cooperative endeavors. For example, in a complex society like ours, we generate laws, rules, customs, taxes, and all sorts of systems that require cooperation. If we tax people, we require some rules about the taxes. If some people believe that cigarettes and booze are "evil", then they might argue to tax these things more heavily than say, a health club membership. This makes a certain amount of sense in the abstract, but specifically, it does not seem to explain much. For example, though America has never been nor is it now a "Christian" nation in the sense of a state sponsored religion, 70% of the population self-identify as "Christian." Although I have forgotten many Bible verses that won me my radium painted glow in the dark cross, I still know that a main message of the New Testament is to love your neighbor as yourself; to turn the other cheek; to do unto others as you would have them do unto you.

Yet, the United States has more billionaires than any other country. And the highest incarceration rate. Odd. Meanwhile, China purports to be a "Communist" country and one of the main tenets of Communism is "from each according to their abilities and to each according to their needs." And China has the *second* highest number of billionaires. So, in these two giant nations, there is a huge disconnect between what people *claim* are central principles guiding their lives and what they *actually choose to do.*

The mystery and science behind seeing double is basically as follows. Our eyes adapt as we look at something near or far. When we look at something far away, our eyes point straight ahead and parallel; aimed at infinity. At the same time, we allow our lenses to "thin" in order to focus each eye at infinity. When I peer out my office window at the ocean, I can tell the ocean is father away than the palm trees because of *other* cues such as interposition (the palm trees partly obscure my view of the ocean so they are closer than the ocean) and aerial perspective (the ocean looks "fuzzier" than the palm trees because there is more distortion due to there being more air between me and the ocean than there is between me and the palm trees). If we look at something close, normally our eyes converge (point inward slightly toward the object) and we focus at the same time; that is, we make the lens thicker. However, we can "train" oneself to separate these two actions. For example, I can converge ("cross") my eyes to look at my nose but accommodate (to the extent I still can) to distance so that objects in the distance look "sharp" — but there are two such images. Even though I am capable of seeing double, I don't walk around seeing double all the time. That would be both impractical and inconvenient.

Perhaps religion is like that for some people. Looking at things from a "Christian" perspective is, for some, something one learns to do at church, but it is too inconvenient or too impractical to keep doing it when it comes to actually interacting with other people. When you meet someone dressed in their "Sunday Finest" and they call you a S*** A**, you act really offended and shocked. But that doesn't mean you can't call them exactly that the other six days of the week. And, if you own a factory where you hire young girls to paint the dials on glow-in-the-dark watches, you can encourage them to use their tongue and lips to repoint the little camel hair brushes that they use. And after a few years, they may not look much like angels any more. But you can still deny that your radioactive paint had anything to do with it. Because, apparently, although Jesus may have said, "Do unto others as you would have them do unto you," that has nothing to do with harming actual human beings in order to maximize profit. It turns out, "Business is business" trumps the Golden Rule. If you're having trouble understanding that, maybe it will help if you learn to cross your eyes. Don't learn to see too clearly though. No, we wouldn't want that.

4 THERE'S A PILL FOR THAT

In the first grade at David Hill Elementary School in Akron, Ohio, a classmate of mine literally broke out in measles right in front of me. Sure enough, a few days later, I got the measles too. I don't recall its being too bad except that I had a high fever and I began seeing "floaters" which I had never noticed before.

Unfortunately, right after getting "over" the measles, I came down with pneumonia and had another high fever. I soon found myself in a hospital ward with 15-20 other kids. Initially, the worst part of the experience was that I had to lie there in what was essentially a crib. I had outgrown a crib years before and it was humiliating to be caged up in a crib.

At that point in time, the medical community had decided that the best thing for everyone concerned was to limit parental visiting hours to a half hour in the middle of the day and an hour in the evening. Although I certainly enjoyed playing with my friends at school, as an only child, I was also fine being on my own for hours at a time. Yet, being deprived of friends or relatives for all but an hour and a half a day felt crushing. None of the kids could touch each other in the hospital but we could talk a little, and sometimes scream. One of the kids in the ward had been badly burned and they periodically came to change his bandages. Before this, I had mainly heard kids scream as a kind of protest or to get attention from their parents or teachers. This guy's screams arose from a different place in his throat and reached an altogether different acoustic plane. His screams were not designed to get sympathy or attention; they weren't "designed" screams at all. If you consider evolution as a kind of "designer," then these screams were "designed" to warn every other member of his species to get the hell away from here as fast as humanly possible. Only we couldn't. We were caged.

Occasionally, a kid would get better and be released from the prison-like hospital ward. Or, perhaps they were let out early for good behavior. I wasn't sure, but I reckoned that good behavior couldn't hurt. I tried, therefore, to lie still for my penicillin shots twice daily. I pretty much failed at that endeavor. It wasn't so much that the shots were painful as that they were invasive. I still hate the idea of a needle with chemicals being plunged into my body. There is a reason, after all, that human bodies come with skin!

I soon discovered, however, that hospitals offer up even worse things than shots. I was admitted late at night and my first morning, a nurse came by and placed a capsule into an empty drinking glass beside my bed. Because I was so "sick" I was only allowed a very soft and bland diet. I did feel sick. But I also felt very much that I would have been capable of eating a hamburger, hot dog, or slice of turkey. But no. I was stuck with jello, gelatin, bouillon and juice. But my first course for the day was my little pill. About a half hour after the first nurse had deposited a capsule in my empty water tumbler, another nurse came by to "give me my meds." She immediately lifted up the pill so carefully laid in the water tumbler.

However, when she picked it up, the capsule stuck and then disintegrated. "No problem," said the nurse cheerily. "We'll give it to you with orange juice." Indeed, she then mixed the contents of the capsule with orange juice. I had to drink it all. And so I did. And it stayed down. For about 30 seconds. Then I threw up. There was something about this particular mixture taken on an empty stomach which I could not stomach. Just thinking about it now still nauseates me more than a half century later.

The next day, before breakfast, a nurse came in and placed a capsule into my empty water glass. I explained to her that this was not a good idea because the second nurse would break it when she tried to lift it up. She pooh-poohed that as nonsense and went on her way. About an hour later, the second nurse came by to give me my meds. I explained to her to be very careful or the capsule would break. "Nonsense," she said, "the capsule won't break." So, she lifted it up and the capsule broke. "No problem," said the nurse cheerily. "We'll give it to you with orange juice." Indeed, she then mixed the contents of the capsule with orange juice. I had to drink it all. And so I did. And it stayed down. For about 30 seconds. Then I threw up. There was something about this particular mixture taken on an empty stomach which I could not stomach.

And, so it went. Every day for ten days the same exact thing happened. Looking back, it is rather amazing I even survived. Eventually, either the doctor gave up on me or my parents missed me or the hospital needed the bed for a patient that provided a higher revenue source. Whatever the reason, I was eventually paroled. It certainly cannot have been for good behavior. My release, whatever the reason, was right before Easter and I weighed 48 pounds at nearly seven years old. We had ham and yams and mashed potatoes and gravy for Easter dinner. I ate and ate. No doubt, the penicillin helped kill the pneumonia germs. But I really think the Easter dinner is what cured me — that, and being home in a warm house rather than caged on a ward with the screams of a burn victim and worse, the friendly banter of nurses who would never listen to a mere kid. There can be no doubt that pills often do cure disease. But sometimes, whatever the scale of the disease, it isn't so much a little pill as a nourishing environment that restores the balance of health.

On today's TV, you can find advertisements for pills that promise to cure every ailment that humanity has ever had, as well as hundreds of other ailments no-one ever realized were ailments. "Do you suffer from wrinkly elbow skin when you straighten your arm? There's a pill for that!" "Calluses making your feet unsightly? There's a cream for that!" "You *are* eighty years old and you *look* eighty years old? No problem! We can fix that with operations and injections!" And, then, whilst someone tip-toes through a sunlit host of golden daffodils with Beethoven's Ode to Joy playing in the background, a rapid recital of side-effects drones happily. "Some patients may experience slight exploding of the liver. Tell your doctor if you have ever had a beer. Cure-it-all isn't for all patients. If you experience sudden blindness, deafness, or death, stop taking Cure-it-all and seek medical help immediately."

No doubt that there have been real advances in medicines for a number of real diseases both deadly and more minor. But how much of our health care costs are really *vanity* costs? You have a body that adapts to the situation. If there are calluses on your feet, there's a reason! Americans food companies spend many millions of dollars on advertising to get small children into the habit of eating lots of refined sugar even though we know this is *really bad* for kids and helps insure that they will overeat and likely be sick in adulthood. Many more millions of dollars are spent on advertising to persuade adults to eat unhealthy foods. Then, millions more are spent to make you think you are a weak-willed blob if you are overweight. Then, millions more advertising dollars are spent to make you think that a pill or potion will make you skinny despite a bad diet — a bad diet that you initially got into largely because of the advertising dollars.

What if people instead spent money and time making really nutritious meals? What if, instead of watching pro football, people went for a hike with their kids? Maybe we wouldn't need quite so many pills, capsules, shots, and operations. Here's the dilemma. Some pills are really useful under certain circumstances for some people. But profits will be greater if those pills are used by *every* person in *every* circumstance. The CEOs of drug companies are paid on the basis of their company's profits. They are *not* paid on the basis of their company's product's effectiveness or of the cost/benefit ratio of their products. Nope. Profit. That's it. If you were the CEO of a drug company and suppressed results about the negative or even deadly side-effects of one of your

profitable drugs, that would be seen as "good business."
If, as CEO, you cornered the market on a class of drugs
and then jacked the price up so that people could no
longer afford a life-saving medicine and nutritious food
and a warm house, bravo! On the other hand, if you were
an employee in a drug company and stole a couple pens,
you would most likely be fired. Most large companies
these days require their employees to take ethics training
which explains, for example, that you shouldn't lie or
steal. Typically, such training is "introduced" by a signed
letter from the CEO explaining how they take ethics very
seriously and that you should too. Clearly, what they
mean by "ethics" is different from what most people
think "ethics" means. What company "ethics" courses are
really aimed at is keeping people who work for the
company from costing the company money. If you sweep
the floor at Pepsi, you'd better not sweep the floor for
Coke as well! That's a conflict of interest. On the other
hand, if you are a millionaire member of the Board of
Directors, hey, no problem if you're on six or seven other
boards!

If a system is broken, it should probably be fixed or
replaced. Unfortunately, doing so is a little more
complicated than just taking a pill. Often, the people
taking actions and making decisions are far removed
from those suffering the consequences. Nurse One puts a
capsule in the bottom of a water glass and rushes off.
Nurse Two comes in later and tries to pull up the capsule
spilling the contents and concocts a nightmare-flavored
orange juice. Orderly One cleans up the mess. Neither
Nurse Two nor Orderly One ever tells Nurse One about

the mistake. Of course, Kid One might mention it day after day, but who cares what a mere kid says?

Imagine a pill called a "Step-Back" pill. If you took this pill, you might actually listen to what a mere kid says. If you took this pill, you might take a look at the whole system of which you were a part. If you took the "Step-Back" pill, you might find yourself questioning why things are done the way they are and how they might be improved. If you took the "Step-Back" pill, you might even find yourself wondering why it is, exactly, that when extremely rich people who head up drug companies and banks cheat millions of people there is no real penalty but if someone robs a drug store, they will likely spend a good portion of their life in prison. Rumor has it that the "Step-Back" pill was actually invented many years ago but the drug companies were too worried about side-effects to attempt bringing it to market.

The most severe side-effect of the "Step-Back" pill is that you may well stop playing the game of behaving so as to damage your own health. But if you did that, you would not have to buy various potions, pills, and capsules to *regain* your health. Why rock the boat? Unfair-Status-Quo is a bitter capsule to swallow, but luckily it's sugar coated. I'll just rest it here at the bottom of your water glass. Someone will be along in an hour or so. They will lift up the capsule and spill the bitter insides into the glass. But you know what is really an excellent emetic when taken on an empty stomach?

5 NANCY THE NURSE

Our second grade teacher at David Hill Elementary School loved contests. I also loved her contests. She ran contests on naming classical pieces of music that she played on a phonograph. I won. She ran contests for knowing facts about the world and about the USA. I won. She ran contests on spelling. I won. She had contests for math facts but I did not win. Why? Because even though I knew all the answers, she didn't call on me so often as she did some of the girls in the class and one of them won. At the time, I thought this wildly unfair though looking back on it, I see that she might have been trying to encourage some of the others not to give up. She ran a reading contest. I won.

Unlike any of the other contests, she promised that whoever won the reading contest would receive a prize from her. That prize consisted of whatever Golden Book the champion desired. Golden Books comprised a series of small books for kids, each bound on the edge with gold. Well, it probably wasn't actual gold, but it was gold in color. The front and back covers were also rimmed with a gold pattern. So, right off the bat, Golden Books were *very cool!* Each Golden Book also featured, on the back cover, a list of *every* Golden Book! What a clever marketing ploy. Anyway, after I won the reading contest, she handed me a Golden Book so I could pick the title of my dreams from the back cover. I scanned the list very carefully. One and only one Golden Book came with merchandise! Yes, *Nancy the Nurse*, the index promised, came with real band-aids!

In order to understand the appeal of this feature, you need to understand where my family lived. Our family's small one-story two bedroom house sat on a busy street. Most of the block contained other small, one-story two bedroom houses like ours although they differed in the color of the roof and the siding. Our house was white with green trim. However, as luck would have it, at the very end of my block were *three* vacant lots! These were not mere fields of weeds or turned up dirt clods like most of the vacant lots in the area. No these were *forested lots.* Huge trees! Grape vines! A few dirt paths criss-crossed this wooded wilderness, this jungle. It was Eden — only better, because *our* Eden lacked any supernatural authority figure or any adult supervision whatsoever.

And therein lay both the beauty and the beastly danger. At the end of the block, in those ancient verdant stands of oak and beech, we lived or died by our own wits every day — well — every day until our parents called us in for supper when it got dark. But meanwhile, we needed to fend for ourselves and prepare for every emergency.

So, a book — that is one thing. But a book that came with *real bandaids*! That meant that I could construct an emergency medical kit for our wilderness adventures! So, of course, I chose as my prize, *Nancy the Nurse*!

When I made my choice, however, my teacher, Miss Hall, looked at me for a moment, paused, and then quietly suggested, "I think you probably mean *Tommy the*

Doctor." She slid her gnarly finger down to show me the title. Well, *Tommy the Doctor* did sound pretty cool. Indeed, my own nickname had once been "Tommy." However, there was nothing in the description of *Tommy the Doctor* that gave even the slightest hint of real bandaids so I said, "No, thanks. I'll take *Nancy the Nurse.*"

My teacher, Miss Hall, paused, raised her voice just a tad and asked, "How about this one? *Mike the Mechanic.*" Clever the way her voice reminded me of victorious trumpets when she mentioned the name. Still, again, there was nothing there about the book being accompanied by a toolkit or indeed even a bandaid. So, again, I repeated, "No, thanks I'll just take *Nancy the Nurse.*" Miss Hall made a few more increasingly desperate attempts but all to no avail. I was puzzled by all of this. She had made it very clear prior to the contest that the winner would be able to chose *any* Golden Book. At last, she grew weary of the game as had I and she took a different tack. "Well, I will have to check with your parents." And so she did. To their credit, my parents had no qualms at all about my choosing *Nancy the Nurse.*

Soon the book came. I do not recall, but I am guessing that I did read the book. I read most everything I could get my hands on. But I recall nothing about the book. It did really come with bandaids however, and I found an old lunch pail to hold my emergency wilderness kit. However, as anyone knows, an emergency survival wilderness kit needs more than bandaids. For example, a method of remote emergency communication could prove vital. Kids back then did not have cell phones; mainly because they had not yet been invented. So, I needed another method. Something brightly colored would be good. In TV shows and movies, someone in danger often shot off a flare gun. Sadly, my parents did not own a flare gun. However, what they did have was a typewriter. And that typewriter had a ribbon with dark black on one half of the strip and a bright red on the other.

My parents never used the typewriter. And they had been very supportive of part one of my plan for the emergency kit; namely, the bandaids. I had no inkling they would be anything less than thrilled by my appropriation of the typewriter ribbon for such a noble cause as mine. I quickly discovered that touching the ribbon directly instantly dyed my fingers. I learned to hold it carefully at the edges while I added the potentially crucial element to our jungle survival kit. Sure enough *the very first day*, I desperately needed to use it. One of the kids found a gigantic caterpillar. I had already shown everyone my "flare" and explained its use. I carefully removed the ribbon from my kit holder, took the ribbon cartridge in my right hand, squatted down, leapt back up and gave a *tremendous* underhand throw. Sure enough, the red and black ribbon deployed beautifully, wavering into the green of the overhanging canopy. Maybe none of the other kids were looking and maybe as a consequence I had to yell to them to come see the caterpillar anyway, but that misses the point. The point is, it had *worked*. I carefully would the ribbon back up for another emergency, being careful to brush off the larger twigs and dirt clods.

I can't recall how long life continued in this idyllic condition, but somewhere along the line, to my great surprise, my parents claimed an interest in using the typewriter. This, in turn, proved difficult precisely because there was no ribbon. They seemed perturbed to learn that while the ribbon was intact; rather than just letting it sit in the typewriter doing nothing for weeks, I had been using it on multiple occasions to send emergency flares into the sky. "Intact" may be too strong a word for the condition in which I returned it. It *was* in one piece, so there was that. On the other hand, the ink distribution had become a bit uneven. This they did not realize until they actually began typing. The ribbon also frankly looked a bit disheveled and dusty, like a teenager coming home early the next morning from prom night. When I had first acquired my "flare gun," the ribbon had borne a striking resemblance to the *beginning* of the prom night with everyone's clothes, hair, and make-up perfectly composed and smiling alert faces everywhere. Now, dissolution ruled.

I also suppose, by adult standards, none of my emergencies really "counted" because my friends and I were never really hurt, lost, or attacked by wild beasts. But *my* point was that if any of those things *had* happened, we were prepared. Thanks to me. But thanks is not what I got. What I got was incredulity. What I got was yelling. What I got was a spanking. What I got was a lecture about not taking things that don't belong to me, at least without asking.

In my parents' minds, the typewriter ribbon was part of the typewriter, pure and simple. They had what I now know is called "functional fixedness." They failed to see that a typewriter ribbon can serve as a typewriter ribbon when needed, but meanwhile can also be used as an excellent flare gun. They seemed to have a similar problem regarding the siding on the house. Yes, it could be used to form a wall that kept warm air in but it could also be used as a partner in a ball game if no-one else was around.

On the other hand, sometimes my parents instead *teamed up* with innovation. They didn't seem to have any problem with my using old cardboard boxes and paper towel rolls to make castles. They didn't object when I used the short Lincoln Logs as soldiers or constructed a canon out of a short one and a medium one. Using marbles as soldiers caused no problems. Using sticks and stones to make homes for toy dinosaurs was okay too. So, I'm not sure "functional fixedness" precisely named their problem. I think our main difference was that I saw things primarily in terms of their uses. Well — especially, *my* uses. Sure, the typewriter ribbon might be an important part of a typewriter, but if no-one ever used the typewriter and therefore never used the ribbon, why not let it become more useful by being an emergency flare gun? If no-one ever actually *wore* the diamond ring in my mother's jewelry box, why not give it to my girlfriend at school instead? My mother found out and marched up to school to demand the ring back, quite rightly pointing out that the ring had not been mine to give away.

Many years later, I discovered that the ring in question was an engagement ring from my mother's first husband. My mother and dad fell in love in college. But when World War Two came to America, my dad lied about his age and volunteered. My mother was both angry and heart-broken. She married another older man who hadn't volunteered to go off and fight a war. Yet, in life's inimical and ironic ways, he was almost immediately drafted and went off to fight the Nazis himself. One day she had Army Officers appear on the doorstep to inform her of his death. Meanwhile, my dad was having his own trials and tribulations. He received a Purple Heart for a shrapnel wound in his shoulder but went back into combat. He and his squad were again shelled and my dad's lower leg was shattered. His buddy was severely wounded and they were under fire so my dad hobbled them to safety further injuring his shattered leg. His fighting days were over and he shipped back to the USA where he and my mother reconciled. She still kept the other guy's ring as a remembrance but never wore it because, after all, she was now married to my dad.

At the time my dad volunteered to go into the Army, he, like most Americans, only knew that we had been attacked at Pearl Harbor and that we were now at war with Germany, Italy, and Japan. Although people were certainly aware of Hitler's rhetoric against Jews and his "White Supremacist" tirades, the full horrors of the concentration camps and pogroms were not revealed until later. Even with all the "alt-right" propaganda of Goebbels, the German leaders may still have been ashamed to let the world know precisely what they were doing. It might seem difficult to believe that the German people didn't know. However, we must remember that one of Hitler's first moves was to eliminate the free press and name Goebbels as his "Minister of Information." Rather than appointing as his second in command someone who actually knew something about how to make Germany more productive and wealthier, Goebbels was primarily tasked with painting a picture of a successful Germany, one that was winning the war. Any small remaining problems were due to a lack of patriotism or the "Jewish Problem."

Of course, I didn't know any of this in the second grade. All I knew was that to be fully effective in our corner jungle, we would have to have a medical kit and a flare. And, I suppose when my dad was under fire in North Africa and in Italy, his unit did have medical kits and flare guns and a lot more besides. But it wasn't enough to prevent hot shrapnel from flying through the air and maiming and killing people. And, today, I honestly don't know what will help keep people safe from the clouds of hate that gather and threaten to hurl us back into another Dark Ages.

Today, we seem to be in a state of emergency but unprepared. The lessons of even recent history seem lost on most of us. You don't need a medical degree to know that some wounds cannot be staunched with bandaids. Flare guns will not remedy a polarized citizenry. We've had signs and signals of danger aplenty — like bombs bursting in air overhead. But these warnings have been dismissed as normal atmospheric disturbances. So that now, after the dictatorial excesses of the late 1930's and early 1940's which led to so many *millions* of deaths —

German, Japanese, Italian, Russian, Canadian, French, English, American and more from virtually every continent, *now* we stand poised to do it all again. We are ready to beat every last one of our plowshares into swords. Many seem sick of science and sick of making progress on disease and understanding the earth or exploring space. Instead, our leaders seem to wallow and wade in the wickedness of self-righteous bigotry. We are ready to fray the very fabric of America and its promise of freedom and equality for all. It feels as though something precious has been given away — something that isn't even ours to give away. It belongs to the humanity and human progress. And, unlike my mom's diamond ring, this stolen gift will not be so easily retrieved.

Of course, you might want to stock up on an extra supply of bandaids or even some of your favorite books. I doubt it will help much, but it can't hurt. If things go badly, the jungle now will not be filled with oak trees and grape vines. And it won't just be a few vacant lots of the end of the block. Vacant lots will waste away on every block as society unravels. Even the lots with massive iron-barred mansions will be populated only by the vacant-eyed. Diamond rings will all have been confiscated as gifts for a chosen few.

And, what of, *Nancy the Nurse,* you ask? Well, Nancy earned her M.D. and became head of surgery at a prestigious University teaching hospital. But when it came right down to her performing life-saving operations, many patients opted instead for Timmy the Technician. Sadly, it turned out that Timmy didn't actually have any technical *or* medical expertise. But he was big and brash and beige. Yes, his patients died but these were deemed *righteous* deaths. Every single death all along that long, loveless lane to a darker destiny will be deemed as just another *righteous* death. And every righteous death will become just another … brick … in … the … wall.

"We don't need no education
We don't need no thought control
No dark sarcasm in the classroom
Teachers leave them kids alone
Hey! Teachers! Leave them kids alone
All in all it's just another brick in the wall
All in all you're just another brick in the wall…"

— Pink Floyd, *Another Brick in the Wall.*

6 STICKS AND STONES

As no less an authority on the universe than George Carlin himself pointed out, parents like to make rules. They supplement these rules with various bits of seemingly sage advice. One of my mom's favorites was "Sticks and stones may break my bones but words will never hurt me." I cannot recall the precise circumstances when I first heard this old saw, but from the very first it bothered me. I have a vague memory, perhaps confabulated, of coming in from outdoor play around the age of six complaining that one of the neighbor kids, probably my best friend Homer, had called me a "bad name." I'm not sure whether I expected mere sympathy or whether I thought my mom would go and extract some sort of retribution. But I didn't get either kind of satisfaction. Instead, I got this saying quoted at me: "Sticks and stones may break my bones but words will never hurt me."

One reason I hated it was that I didn't find hearing this at all *satisfying* (like a hug would have been) and certainly not in the self-righteous and smug way that having Homer being punished would have been. Was this the harbinger of a new chapter in parent-child relationship? (No, I probably didn't use the word "harbinger" back then, but I knew what "change" meant.) Instead of *comfort*, my parents would now dispense *wisdom*? Beyond that, this particular saying hurt my artistic sensibility. "Sticks and stones may break my bones." Now, there was a rhyme scheme and a rhythmic scan I

could relate to. Nice even rhythm. Nice rhyme.
Alliteration and assonance. But then it all goes to hell.
"But words will never hurt…me." ? How does that end
with "hurt me." Which syllable is unaccented? And what
does "me" rhyme with here? You may as well just jam
your piano hand down on C,D,E,F, and G at the same
time and maybe the black keys between as well. By the
way, my parents absolutely objected to that latter action
on my part. I had to play piano "nicely" or not at all.

Beyond that assault on my childhood sense of poetry, the
"message" of this aphorism appeared cloudy if not
opaque. Was my mother suggesting that if I wanted to
"get back at" my buddy Homer, I should not come to her
with my complaints but find a way to break his bones —
perhaps using sticks and stones? I couldn't see myself
doing that. Even then I knew broken bones took a long
time to heal. If I broke his bones, it could interfere with
baseball, hide and seek, cops and robbers, cowboys and
"Indians." Perhaps "words can never hurt me" provided
the crux of the message and the sticks and stones were
just there for contrast effects. Taken by itself, "words can
never hurt me" seemed patently absurd. If I hadn't felt
hurt, I wouldn't have bothered to tell her about it.

Even at six, the logic implied by this aphorism had
offended my sense of form even more than the poetry.
Yeah, true enough, sticks and stones *might* break your
bones. That made sense. But that didn't mean that these
were the *only* weapons of bodily destruction. I already
knew people could get hurt by guns, knives, cars, and
disease. Why are the sticks and stones there at all? Why
not just say, "If someone calls you a name, just ignore

it."? Too subtle for a young child might be, "If someone calls you a name, whether or not that hurts you depends on how you take it." Yeah, I might use that today in psychotherapy with adults. I don't think it would make much sense to a six year old. At least, I don't think it would have made much sense to *me* as a six year old.

As I mentioned, the sticks and stones part did make sense. Yet, I found it surprising that my mom would even mention them as possibilities. Whenever she — or any of the other moms — found us "sword fighting" with sticks, they would warn us that someone was about to lose an eye. This sounded extremely scary and yet a little intriguing. How could you "lose" your eye? Wouldn't you just use your other eye to go find it? Did they mean you could have your eye *injured*? Anyway, none of us had the least intention of trying to stab someone else's eye. And we would certainly prevent our own eye from being stabbed. So what was the problem? It seemed as though adults found it very difficult to say what they actually meant. When it came to rock fights, parents seemed to focus on the same concern — losing an eye. Almost all of the boys I knew participated in both "sword" fights with sticks and in rock fights. Yet, none of us had ever lost an eye. In school, I searched the faces of kids from every grade (up to sixth) and none of the kids in the entire school had ever lost an eye. So, this seemed to me, and apparently all the other boys, to be a rather far-fetched fear.

Indeed, we not only didn't try to blind each other; none of us tried even to break a bone. We *did* try to inflict *some* damage on each other; we did want to make it "hurt" but not enough to break a bone. The little damage we rained on each other mostly constituted collateral damage. Our main purpose: re-enact the "battles" we had seen on TV. Drama, not pain, and certainly not injury, provided our main source of joy when it came to fights. When we played "Cowboys and Indians" or "Cops and Robbers" we had no intention of putting a bullet through someone's heart.

Even the nicely rhyming first part of that aphorism disturbed me. It hinted to me that a far meaner and crueler world existed out there. In that world, kids didn't just want to throw stones and hit with sticks in order to have some dramatic fun; in *that* world, kids actually *wanted* to break each other's bones! What neighborhood was that? I had occasionally heard my parents and grandparents talk about "tough neighborhoods." Were those neighborhoods the ones where kids wanted to break each other's bones? What would be the point? Wouldn't that just make the other kids less fun to play with? If they had a broken leg, they couldn't run. If they had a broken arm, they'd have to swing the bat with one hand. It made zero sense to me. *Zero.*

The application of any term leaves gray areas. We like to think that definitions are clear-cut, but seldom indeed does nature provide us with chip chop clarity when it comes to classes and definitions. For example, is a baseball bat a "stick"? Sometimes, baseball players refer to their bats as sticks, but in the case of well-muscled professional ball players, I always thought they were joking. Indeed, with a (mere) "stick" they can hit a baseball well over 300 feet! But, after all isn't a baseball bat a kind of "stick"? It's made of wood. It's more or less in the shape of a branch of wood.

Well, whether you call it a "stick" or a "bat", I can tell you that when a baseball bat gets swung at you and hits you in the chest full force, it is more than a little painful. Homer managed this deed. We were playing baseball with nearly a full set of players down the block at a vacant lot. Homer was at bat with my ebony black baseball bat and my dad drove up to the edge of the field and shouted at me that we had to go immediately. I walked over to get my bat but Homer stood resolute in the batter's box. The pitcher threw and before I could back away, Homer swung the bat, swinging for the fences. Despite his name, Homer did not hit a home run or even a foul tip. He completely missed the ball although he did manage to make extremely solid contact with my sternum and ribs. It hurt. It hurt quite a bit actually, but the scarier part was that I could no longer breathe. My dad came hurtling through the vacant lot despite his war-wounded leg and grabbed the bat from Homer. I still couldn't breathe but I could tell I was still alive, at least for now. I wasn't so sure whether Homer or I would be the first to visit the great beyond. My dad had a very hot temper and, hit or no-hit, the idea that he would kill Homer sprang into my head and scared me even more than the prospect that I would never be able to breathe again.

Indeed, I did breathe again (as should be obvious) but did get to spend some long hours in the "emergency room" waiting for X-rays. Nothing was broken. Homer and I stopped hanging out. Eventually, Homer's dad came to talk with me and explained that it was an accident. He pointed out that Homer and I played together a lot and we were both missing out. Forgiving Homer seemed pretty easy actually. I myself hated (and *still* hate) to leave a game half finished or lose a turn at bat. In baseball, you only *rarely* get to bat. If full teams are playing, you only get to bat one out of 18 times! We seldom had a full complement of players in my neighborhood, but it was still rare that we got a chance at bat.

Indeed, "sticks" *can* break your bones, although luck sided with me that day and no ribs were broken. It could have been worse. Much worse. The red mark of the bat lay directly over my heart. I suppose a piece of rib could have gone shooting into my heart which would have cut my baseball career short. But while we are on the subject of hearts, how can anyone say, "words will never hurt you"? Of course, it hurts when people call someone a hurtful name. Kids call each other names. When they do it on purpose, they are generally doing it *precisely* to hurt the other kid. That isn't universally true. As I already explained, when I had met my neighbor a few years ago and called her a S***A**, I had no idea what it meant. It was just her way of saying hello. And, sometimes, even adults call people names or comment on their appearance and although it is meant as a compliment, it is not taken as one.

For example, when I was very young, I had a hard time gaining weight even though I wanted to. This is certainly no longer true; now, I have the opposite problem. But I still don't take kindly to people (generally women) calling me "skinny." In fact, I can't think of any guy I know who wants to be called "skinny" but some women seem to think it's a compliment. As we know, men are far more likely to say various things to women that are not appreciated than *vice versa*. Most guys would *love* to be called "sexy" and find it difficult to understand why a woman would not just take this as a compliment. That's basically because guys are typically taken "seriously" while women have to fight their whole lives to be taken seriously; that is, to be treated as a person with intelligence, goals, a unique viewpoint and so on and not simply as a "thing" whose main purpose is to please men and propagate the species.

In addition, women face the additional fear, much more often than men, that such a "compliment" is actually a sign of danger; that this "complimenter" is really precisely the kind of jerk who won't take "no" for an answer, follow them home and engage in other potentially dangerous behavior. Even if there is no danger of a sexual assault, such "compliments" are often anything but and are simply meant to grab power by demeaning the *substance* of what a woman says or does. "Oh, my, you're so *cute* when you're angry (that you didn't get the promotion you deserved)."

Imagine that you overhear a guy saying something that is clearly meant to be derogatory to a woman. What would *you* do? Whether you are a man or a woman yourself, I guarantee that you will not win many points if you walk up to the woman right away and say, "Sticks and stones may break my bones, but words will never hurt me." I don't recommend it. I especially don't recommend it if the woman happens to have a large stick or stone in her possession.

Now, let's imagine instead that there is one particular guy who makes a habit out of calling people derogatory names. He calls many women derogatory names on many occasions. In fact, whenever anyone disagrees with him about anything, he calls that person something derogatory. In fact, name-calling seems to be the most sophisticated type of argument he can muster. In school, we had a few kids that occasionally acted like this and we had a name for them as well: "bullies." The few kids who were "bullies" were never very popular. They were pretty much outcasts.

Bullies act nothing like heroes. A bully is typically driven by a deep fear of being nothing. Quite probably, their parents either spoiled them silly or beat them senseless or called them many hurtful names. Bullies have no self-esteem. When things don't go their way or someone disagrees with them, it brings up deep feelings of inadequacy. The only mechanism that they have for dealing with these feelings is to try to overpower the opposition. They lie, steal, and cheat and scream bloody murder until they get their way. Sometimes in grade school, a bully would be particularly strong physically, but it wasn't really a necessity. In junior high and high school, a student might be a "bully" who would go about name calling and power trips in a different way. Sometimes a whole gang of kids would get together and be bullies together. Their idea of a fun time was to pick a fight where the odds were five to one or ten to one. The whole gang would beat up someone because that way they could insure a win. Unless something happens to change such a person fundamentally, they often graduate from being a child bully to being a teen bully in a gang to being a criminal in a criminal gang.

But not always. Sometimes such folk end up being a "boss." They don't primarily work as a boss because they like to make good things happen. No, they enjoy being the boss because they can order other people around. Sometimes such people even end up as police, politicians or professors and what they enjoy most about the job is ordering other people around. Because they have no confidence in their ability to solve problems or, indeed, do anything productive, they shake down others who can actually produce things. Now, please understand that most bosses just want to get things done and most police really do want to help and protect people. The "bullies" in these positions are a minority. Sometimes, the bullies grow up to be wife beaters or child beaters or child molesters. On rare occasions, they become dictators. In this role, they use their power for one purpose: to enhance their power. We all enjoy having things our way, but the bully feels things *must* be their way. They enjoy shouting down their opposition. They enjoy getting rid of their opposition. They cannot stand the idea that they may be wrong or lacking in some ability.

To give just one example, consider the case of Altshuller, a Russian who invented a way of inventing called TRIZ. (You can find it easily on Google). He was a Russian inventor who wrote a sincere letter to Stalin suggesting that Russians needed to be more inventive. To the thin-skinned bully Stalin, this suggestion for how to *improve*

Russia morphed into an implied criticism and Altshuller was sent to Siberia where he got to cut trees into sticks and break rocks into stones.

Bullies all have (at least) one fatal and common flaw. They cannot face facts and instead insist on their own version of the truth. They cannot learn from their mistakes because they disavow all error on their part. At long last, every such bully becomes more and more dissociated from reality. Essentially, they become insane, but they are not called by that name, because no-one wants to go to Siberia. No-one wants to give them an honest assessment of a military situation so, despite their military ambitions and initial successes, they ultimately must fail. Of course, on the way to their personal failures, such people become responsible for many additional deaths. They would sentence millions to die rather than face their own fundamental inadequacy.

A bully like Stalin or Hitler, however, cannot possibly be a nation-wide bully without arousing the little inner bully in many of his countrymen. Stalin himself didn't personally put 50 million of his own countrymen to death nor did Hitler kill six million Jews with his bare hands. Each had to rely on the actions of many "sub-bullies"; people who would carry out the Uber-Bully's wishes or face the consequences (which, without the collaboration of many of his countrymen would be nothing; but with the collaboration of other sub-bullies would be significant, even deadly). So, here we have an interesting conundrum. The bully wants absolute power but cannot actually achieve that power without the active cooperation of hordes of other sub-bullies. The dictator needs to set up a system to help him be the biggest bully he can be. Without that help, he is forced to face up to how weak and powerless he is personally.

These types of national bullies have arisen many times in many eras and in many different nations. So we cannot blame the "Russians" or the "Germans" or the "Spanish" or the "French" or the "English" as being a nation of people who succumb to the temptation of being a sub-bully. The sub-bully joins right in on the name calling, the stone throwing and the stick wielding but that surrender of one's humanity is not limited to any one nation. Nope. Too easy. And too inaccurate. We all need to look within to discover how and why we might ourselves become a sub-bully and then to determine how to thwart that tendency. If you and I would like to become something *other* than sub-bullies, we need to appreciate our own unique perspectives and abilities and celebrate them. As professor Mad-Eye Moody[1] once famously said, "constant vigilance." Look for opportunities to give, to cooperate, to provide, to learn, to commit acts of compassion and kindness to every person regardless of what they are called. Just forget the sticks and stones. After all, someone could lose an eye.

---

[1] Character from J.K. Rowlings *Harry Potter* books and films beginning with *Harry Potter and the Goblet of Fire, (2000),* New York: Scholastic.

7 THE CRABS ARE BITING!

My dad led the design team for the electrical system on the original Goodyear Blimp (a lighter than air craft; a kind of fancy hot air ballon that can be a serious means of transportation and weaponry). One summer, between the third and fourth grade, Dad's work on airships called him away from Akron and we spent the summer in Tom's River, New Jersey. After returning from Portugal, we had stuck close to Akron so I was eager for a trip that took us hundreds of miles to the seaside. I could smell the ocean when we were still an hour away from Tom's River. Our small apartment in Tom's River sat a mere two blocks from the public library, a library that contained the *Powers of Ten* book which takes the reader on a journey from the innermost workings of the atomic nucleus to the outermost regions of the galaxy.

While my dad worked at Lakehurst, my mom and I spent part of the day watching the "McCarthy Hearings" on TV. I was too young to understand it thoroughly, but even as a nine year old, I could quickly discern that McCarthy was a liar. I had a harder time telling whether he was genuinely a very hateful person or whether he just appeared to be full of hate in order to be popular with other hating people. Hating others has never come very naturally to me. I always felt connected to my family, my friends, other people and even other forms of life. So, hating, to me, has always consisted of nine parts self-loathing plus one part prideful ignorance. Don't get the idea that I am a saint. I'm far from it and anger comes quite easily to me when I'm frustrated. My parents claimed that, as a toddler, frustration would propel me to run across the room and smack my head down on the floor. By the time I was nine, I had developed less self-destructive ways to express anger. Whether McCarthy really was a tiny person filled with hate or simply a person who tried to impress those who really were haters in order to win their support, I couldn't tell. I have no idea how large McCarthy was physically. I call him tiny because it seems to me essential that in order to hate, you must shrink your sense of wonder and appreciation to the boundaries of your own physical skin. When people hate, something undesirable has happened to them and they feel that it absolutely shouldn't have happened to them because, after all, they are the center of their very small universe. Apparently, haters have never seen the book, *Powers of Ten*. Such a book might have given McCarthy and others of his ilk an appreciation for how they are actually part of something far grander than a single human ego.

Perhaps to garner some adult time for themselves, my parents also enrolled me in summer church school. I became friends with one of the kids in church school and he invited me onto his Cabin Cruiser for crab fishing. My parents met with his parents before allowing me to accept this offer and they ended up also being invited. A bright sunny day and off we sped onto the sparkling ocean! At some point, we kids, under the supervision of my new friend's dad, began crab fishing. Although I had never gone crab fishing before, I understood the basic concept from several fishing trips with my Uncle Karl. Karl lived in a modernized log cabin on the shore of

Comet Lake, a suburb of Akron. Fishing, in my experience, had consisted of going out onto the lake in a row boat, putting a live worm onto a hook, putting a fishing pole over the side of the boat and then sitting quiet and still for hours on end. I think I may have caught one small fish in my three trips with Uncle Karl. It seemed frankly like a *huge* amount of boredom for a very small reward. So, when crab fishing was announced as the next activity on the Cabin Cruiser, I steeled myself for hours of boredom. I didn't want to end up running across the deck and smacking my head in frustration.

The baiting was easier and instead of poles, we put out some lines with multiple baits. Over the side of the boat they went. That wasn't so bad as pithing the worms. Now I imagined would come the endless hours of waiting for a nibble. Two or three minutes later, for no reason I could discern, we started pulling up the lines. They were filled with crabs! While the trout, bass, perch, and bluegill in Comet Lake were shy and crafty little critters who would stealthily nibble away the worm without getting barbed on the hook, the crabs of the Atlantic seemed to have no greater goal in life than to clamber into our boat as fast as possible. This fishing sped along more in synch with my natural rhythm. No need for head-banging here! Line after line went over the side and minutes later, back each one would come with a meal's worth of crabs. *This* kind of fishing was more like it!

After sunset had scattered its scarlet shards across both the sky and the Atlantic, we kids went down below to sleep in the bunks. There were portholes in the bow and we could see through those portholes into an ever-darkening starry sky. We could hear the murmuring of the alcohol-plied adults above buzz-talking about whatever it was that adults discussed back then; perhaps the McCarthy Hearings; perhaps something about a popular movie or TV show. We kids below had more serious things to understand. Mainly, we discussed the fact that we could see stars that were (or at least had been) far, far away. We speculated whether, at this very moment, there might be a planet circling one of those distant stars (this was long before the actual discovery of exoplanets). It seemed to us that if there were planets, those planets might also have oceans and Cabin Cruisers and kids. And those kids might well be looking up into the night sky seeing what appeared to them as a faraway star — our sun! And, those alien kids might well be thinking of how there might be a planet circling Sol and how on that planet could be kids looking up at the night sky at them…or at least at their sun. Of course, we might be years or even thousands of years "out of synch" in our mutual gazing — which only added to the mystery.

These possible aliens might be like us in every way. More likely, they would be like us in some ways and unlike us in some ways. They might be wondering whether we would be friendly to them just as we wondered whether they would be friendly to us. And, probably, we concluded, a lot would depend on the particular alien you encountered. For some reason, that particular small group of kids didn't talk much about "categories" of people. It seemed to me, and to my new-found friends, that everyone was quite different. We had learned in school that every snowflake was different. If something as simple as a snowflake is unique, how much more true that must be of people. And, it seemed completely and obviously true. My Aunt Emma and my Aunt Mary were completely different from each other as each was from my Grandmother Ada. Of course, people were *all* different. As I listened to the voices of the other kids, I could see that kid's face in my mind's eye. Yes, we all had one nose, one mouth, and two eyes, but we were all really different. We sounded different. We looked different. We moved differently. We were from different states hundreds of miles apart. But we all were interested in whether there were aliens and what they would be like. Though we were somewhat mindful of the potential danger of an alien invasion, we were much more excited about learning about them and from them than we were in protecting ourselves from them. And we all understood that all the thoughts and feelings we were having about them were quite possibly mirrored by their thoughts and feelings about us even if separated by lightyears of space-time and by our separate biological lineages.

None of our group of nine-year olds were such "scaredy cats" that we were terrified of the aliens and therefore filled our hearts with hate for them. It never occurred to any of us. I don't think that's just because we were all going to "church school." It was just more natural to assume that the kids on the faraway planet would be wondering about us in much the same way as we wondered about them regardless of the number of eyes and legs they might have. I think that in order for us to have hated or feared the aliens, an adult would have to come into our cramped quarters to tell us that all aliens were the same; that they were all out to *get us*; that they should all be hated and destroyed. Maybe McCarthy would be good for that job. It's honestly hard to believe any of us would have taken him seriously. But, I suppose, if we heard that hate spouted day in and day out, complete with fake news features filled with fake facts and fake figures, we might eventually find ourselves in a state of hate and fear.

Of course, no such adult came down below decks to sell us that particular bogus bill of bads. Why would someone like McCarthy decide to make their fame and fortune by filling young minds and hearts with hate and fear? I still don't know whether he was really so filled with hate and fear himself that he couldn't help it. I did, years later, read a biography of Joe McCarthy and something his wife was quoted as saying in that book made me think it was all just a ploy for power and that he didn't *actually* believe *any* of it. That just makes it all the more disturbing. A hate-monger such as McCarthy, who does it all as an act to gain power, does not just hate communism and communists. *He also hates the people he is hoodwinking*. He totally disrespects them through his dishonesty and dissembling. Eventually, Joe McCarthy soon found himself completely discredited and disgraced but not before wantonly laying waste to the lives of many innocent individuals. Why would anyone do such a thing? It was incomprehensible then and it remains incomprehensible to me, even to this day.

Of course, in the right circumstances, almost everyone lies on occasion. What most people do when they are caught in a lie is apologize and try to explain why they lied. What the McCarthys of the world do, however, is quite different. Instead of apologizing, they simply shout

the lie more and more loudly. Sometimes, they will deny
ever having told the lie in the first place (even if they
have been taped!). Their screaming gets louder and
louder. When no-one else believes their lies, their only
recourse is violence. War, incarceration, murder — all of
these seem as nothing compared with the ego bruising
hurt of admitting that they had been lying. In the
meantime, Joe McCarthy did provide a summer's worth
of entertainment. It's too bad it came with ruining so
many innocent lives.

Now, today, I wonder whether those far planets we
hypothesized as revolving around those far suns in our
night sky have their own McCarthy-like beings. It seems
hard to believe an entire species would survive if they
were *all* McCarthy-like. Imagine a river full of piranha
that attacked each other! The species wouldn't long
survive. Is there some utility to having a small proportion
of the population of an otherwise intelligent species be
McCarthy-like? I don't really think so. At least I haven't
been able to come up with a scenario in which hate-
mongering is useful to the group as a whole, though I can
imagine it provides some short term excitement.

A related phenomenon might be called "Cassandra-like"
in which someone thinks they see a danger which no-one
else does. But such a person is useful to the society as a
whole only to the extent that they are willing to share
their concern and work together with others to determine
whether the danger is real, how to assess it, how to
protect against it, etc. On the other hand, if the person
simply insists that there is a danger regardless of whether
others see it and they try to "prove" it by screaming more

loudly, that is not very helpful. In the case of McCarthy, the "danger" was premised on something which is absurd on its face. For instance, McCarthy held that if you were friends with a communist, that meant you must be communist as well; or, because some communists wanted to overthrow the US government, if you were a communist, that meant *you* also wanted to overthrow the US government. Such thinking cannot lead to very effective action. A McCarthy-like person is completely *unhelpful* in locating and protecting against *actual* danger because their cognition is too damaged to be helpful in itself and their communication style is so warped that it actively interferes with the attempts of others to solve real problems.

In the years after that summer of McCarthyism, I worked with kids in many capacities. For instance, I worked as a child care worker and camp counselor. I can tell you that kids often engage in conversations about deep topics. They are concerned about their world and other worlds that might be. Kids care passionately to learn about the world. But despite their passion, they tend to be pretty careful about discriminating the bait from the hook. In my experience, they are more like the Comet Lake trout, perch, bass, and bluegill than were the crabs off the New Jersey coast. However, if people of any age are desperate enough; if they are told the big lie often enough, many will stop acting like discerning vertebrate fish and just latch on to the first shiny thing that appears before them. Perhaps that is why the McCarthys of the world, if they had their way, would outlaw public libraries, gut public education, and discredit the independent press. They would not want the fish to be able to discriminate the bait from the hook. They are much too impatient for trout fishing. Their idea of a good time is to simply toss a line over the side of the boat and make sure that people are so desperate that they clamp right onto the empty hooks. Who knows what exactly goes on in the mind of a crab? Perhaps they clamp on in hate. Perhaps they latch on in fear. Perhaps it is a little of both. What we do know is that whatever motivates the crab to grab hold of that shiny line, it is always the crab itself, not its imagined enemies, who ends up in the belly of the beast.

8 PARAMETRIC RECIPES AND AMERICAN DEMOCRACY

Most people are familiar with the concept of a recipe. It lists a set of proportions or amounts of various ingredients and the steps that should be taken in producing a compound food item for consumption. The goal of a recipe is to encapsulate a "best practice" which has been developed over time. Following the steps is important for a good result. If you cook a cake too little, it will be gooey but if you cook it too much, it will be dry or even burned. If you stray from the correct proportions of sugar or flour, say, the resulting cake will not be as good in terms of texture, taste, or both.

If you do stray from a recipe, there are often many ways to go wrong. My mother used to make peanut butter cookies. Homemade peanut butter cookies still warm from the oven still call to me from every room in the house. As a kid, they even drew me in from playing outside! And, this wonderful taste treat was repeated every time…except for the time that Mom accidentally put in salt instead of sugar. Randomly replacing one ingredient with another typically results in a recipe — for disaster.

A "parameter" is something that can be changed from one situation to another. While randomly changing ingredients does not often work, there are many recipes which allow for huge flexibility among some of their ingredients. For example, I often make a salad for lunch. On top of the fresh vegetables and greens, I use pepper and one teaspoon of olive oil along with one teaspoon of balsamic vinegar. But which greens and vegetables are in these salads?

That depends. In every salad, I include vegetables according to which ones are the freshest. I also include a variety of colors. To me, a green salad that is all green is not so attractive as one with bits of color. Adding red peppers, radishes, tomatoes, yellow peppers, carrots, red onion, radicchio, or cheese makes it more appealing. To some extent, that is probably just because variety itself is interesting. Beyond that, people may react to the bright colors that typically signal important and biologically useful phytochemicals. While people have long known the value of vegetables, more recent research has confirmed that brightly colored fruits and vegetables often contain substances that help prevent cancer, among other benefits.

A salad is more interesting, at least to me, if there is a variety of textures as well as colors and tastes. Carrots, cucumbers, tomatoes, lettuce and snap peas all have quite different textures and this variety adds to the pleasure of the salad. So, when I "create" a salad, I take care to include a variety of textures as well as colors and tastes. The only substances which are "measured" are the olive oil and vinegar. I do not need to follow a strict recipe regarding the vegetables. Since I typically shop and prepare food only for two people, I need to "use up" ingredients while they are still fresh. Indeed, my choices are often even more complicated. I know from experience approximately how long various vegetables will still be fresh and so choose, not just the very freshest, but also vegetables that are fresh today but may not be so tomorrow. Parametric recipes, when appropriate, prevent boredom; such recipes can be both economical and healthy.

Salads are not the only example of a "parametric recipe." I also use such a scheme for making an omelet. My omelet always contains eggs and cheese but could include any number of various vegetables. There are "constraints" on the vegetables. I would not typically make an omelet with only hot peppers, onions, and garlic for example, because it would be too hot for my taste. I use a variety for color and texture, but to a large extent, the omelets I make are never the same twice. I also use a variety of cheeses. I suppose if I had access to numerous types of eggs, I could also vary the egg type but I do not do that in practice. Other common "parametric recipes" include stews, soups, fried rice, beans and greens, curried vegetables, baked potato with vegetable/cheese toppings, burritos, tacos, fruit salads, bean salads, and pizza. To be sure, some parts of these "recipes" are more parametric than others. The pizza dough must be prepared according to much stricter "rules" than the selection and proportion of toppings.

As mentioned earlier, many recipes *do* require very strict adherence. Many recipes for baking must be followed closely in terms of ingredients, proportions, and the steps taken in preparation. Even more vitally, you do not want your pharmacist improvising when they compound your prescriptions. In other words, there are cases where parametric recipes are extremely useful and practical. There are other situations where strict adherence to recipes is better. And, there are many situations where certain aspects of the recipe require strict adherence while other aspects of the same recipe can be varied quite a bit. When you use a parametric recipe, some attention is required along the way. Simply adding different vegetables to an omelet or salad will always add variety, but for best results, you need to *think* about what you are adding in order to optimize color, texture, etc. as well as individual tastes. While my wife and I both love kale, collard greens, garlic, onions, mushrooms, and cilantro, for example, I know that not everyone likes these ingredients so when making an omelet for a guest, I enquire about their preferences for the vegetables and cheeses that I incorporate.

What does the culinary conundrum of "parametric recipes" have to do with American Democracy?

Everything.

Anarchy is much like grabbing a handful of ingredients that are closest at hand and simply throwing them in a pot and cooking them for a random period of time. There is no structure and there is no learning from best practices and there is no accountability. On the other hand, fascism is like finding one recipe you like, if you are the one in power, and insisting that *everyone* like it because *you* like it. Imagine you were a guest in my house and I insisted you eat my blue cheese and shiitake mushroom omelet even though you hated blue cheese and hated mushrooms. I could say, "Well it's my house! Eat what I make!" Some people were pretty much brought up that way. At the other extreme, some parents will end up making four omelets for four different kids because they want to please everyone. With infinite time and resources, this may not be a horrible way to go. However, you may be surprised to learn that most people do *not* have infinite time and resources. So, when it comes to making an omelet for four very different people some compromise may be necessary. Indeed, in some cases, omelets may not be the best option.

The problem with a purely fascist approach is not simply that it is mean and mean-spirited. It is far worse than that. First of all, if you never get the omelet you want (or indeed any omelet you can even stomach) eventually, you are going to try to "overthrow" the damned chef and make your own omelet. You might not like omelets at all and prefer cereal for breakfast. In "normal" American Democracy, that's fine. I can make an omelet for myself and you can have cereal. But if I have forced you to eat omelets for a year even though you hate them, you can bet that once *you* are in power, you'll be forcing me to eat your ridiculous cereal for at least a year. Fascism leads to power grabs and ultimately to violence.

A second problem with fascism is that only a very few people in power are really happy with the results. Imagine that those in power force their "optimal recipe" omelet on everyone all the time and more and more people get sick of it over time. The people in power, I suppose, get some kind of pleasure from "forcing" their will on everyone else, but it is nothing compared with the pleasure that normal people get from creating something that "works" for all the people involved. Fascism is not about love, cooperation, or pleasure. It feeds on fear, hate, and meanness. It doesn't really matter whether the fascism has some quasi-religious affiliation (like the Taliban who outlaw music and trees) or some racial bias like Hitler's Germany. Such a regime is not conducive to people's pleasure (at least not for the vast majority).

Third, fascism is ultimately not very practical. At first, it might seem "efficient." Someone in power gets the "best" recipe for an omelet and then everyone has to fall in line and eat that kind of omelet whether or not it tastes good. If the omelet demands asparagus as the only vegetable, then the entire supply chain can be geared toward asparagus. Efficient! But only under extremely limited circumstances. Suppose that the lack of crop rotation and variety helps cause an asparagus mold plague. Asparagus first becomes very expensive and then non-existent. Or, suppose a foreign agent, knowing everyone has to eat asparagus, finds a way to poison the supply chain. Now, instead of only a few people dying from the poison, everyone will. Or, suppose science discovers that asparagus actually causes kidney stones. Even worse, fascism hates change. In order to prevent change, fascism hates news, science, opinion variety, free speech etc. So, under fascism, when science discovers that the state-approved asparagus is actually poisonous or causes kidney stones, rather than changing the omelet recipe, fascism imprisons the scientist who discovered the problem and tortures him or her until they recant their findings. Problem solved! Recipe unchanged! Efficient! But meanwhile, people are dying from being required to use the recipe.

If everyone were an island unto themselves, there would be no information sharing and people would have to come up with their own omelet recipes. Instead, imagine a world in which people trade recipes informally, are free to discuss, restaurants introduce people to a variety of tastes, people write, publish and read cook books. In that world, people are free to improvise, experiment, find what works, share the information, cater to the situation of what's available, cater to their specific guests, and so on. All this culinary activity is carried out in a very broad context of rules that cannot be broken without penalty. You cannot willingly poison your guests with your omelet. If you do, you'll be carted off to the slammer. You cannot even cook in peanut oil when you know your guest is allergic to peanut oil. People are not allowed knowingly to sell you tainted eggs. This is a good system. That system is, essentially, American Democracy. We have collectively decided that some rules are necessary. (Don't poison people). But we don't demand that everyone use the same recipe. We don't demand that everyone eat the same food. We do not try to enforce our preferences on other people, even when we have the power to do so.

To me, the advantages of a Democracy over Fascism are so obvious that I never imagined for an instant that we might get rid of Democracy in America in favor of Fascism. But Democracy is always on the edge of danger. Imagine what would happen if we were to elect to an office with power, (e.g., POTUS) a mean-spirited egomaniacal Clown who wants to tell us what to eat, whose clothing to wear, what facts we're allowed to pay attention to, who we are allowed to be friends with, who we can have sex with, and who we can marry.

Democracy would not die instantly, but it would be severely wounded. The Clown would have limited powers so long as Congress had the guts to limit the powers of the Clown. We would all need to learn which people in Congress are "ours" and make sure they rein in the Clown immediately. Anyone who failed to do that would need to be voted out as soon as possible and never elected to any public office ever again. Even if you agreed with some of the Clown's executive orders, you would hopefully understand that without a Congress willing to check the Clown, the Clown becomes the Dictator. The Clown would surrounded itself with people who are chosen because it believes such people will enhance its power irrespective of whether they have the slightest experience or ability to do the job. You would have to do what you could to make your Congress accountable to *you.* If you let the Congress be accountable only to the Clown, then you'd be dooming your children and your children's children to live in a Fascistic Circus run by a demented Clown. And, in another four years, you would have *no say* in Congress. And, you'd be required to eat the omelet made with rancid cheese, moldy asparagus, and bad eggs.

Every morning.

Forever.

9 BIG ZIG ZAG CANYON

Ever since I can remember, I have enjoyed hiking. Where I grew up, in Northeastern Ohio, woods, fields, streams and hills provided the typical backdrop. I cannot deny that every new vista, every turn of the path still thrills me with a coursing-through-your-body pleasure…unless of course, the path becomes actually dangerous rather than simply breathtaking. People differ a lot on where that boundary lies between thrilling and insanely stupid. Personally, I find that I get plenty of "adrenaline rush" simply from being a driver or pedestrian or cyclist or playing tennis. Walking across a fallen log 50 feet above a rocky ravine has never been my idea of a good time. I would, of course, try it if *necessary* but I wouldn't enjoy it. On the other hand, speaking in public has always seemed pleasurable although it is definitely nerve-wracking. In any case, it has always seemed to me that there are millions of interesting, beautiful, unique paths, just in America's own 50 states — paths that have very little intrinsic danger. Other countries typically have a panoply of fantastic views and hikes of their own. All of them are worth pursuing.

I never saw "real" mountains until I visited the west coast of America. I hiked a few times on Mt. Rainier with my brothers-in-law. When some of them attended college at Reed in Portland, we decided to take a hike on Mt. Hood in order to take advantage of a clear day. The odd thing about climbing a mountain, at least in the Pacific northwest is that your view of the mountain typically becomes more and more obscured as you come closer to the parking lot where you begin your journey. By the time you park, you actually possess zero sensory evidence that you are anywhere near a mountain. One believes it must be somewhere nearby because of your general orientation in space as well as because of the belief that society is generally cooperative. It has therefore provided *actual* rather than *false* trails, accurate rather than false maps, compasses that actually work rather than ones designed to mislead.

Imagine instead that we lived in a society where it was more common to make false trails than real ones; a society where it was more common to publish false maps than real ones; a society where compasses were all digital — and regularly hacked. Would you still bother to try to climb a mountain for pleasure? At the very least, you would need to construct a completely different strategy.

For our actual hike on Mt. Hood, however, we luckily lived in a society wherein we could generally trust people. We had a map and headed out for what we estimated to be a hike that would get us back to the car right before dark. We were not attempting the summit, but it certainly appeared to be a serious hike. We were basically doing a kind of helical partial circumference trek. The scenery began as spruce and pine gradually gave way to more scrub and less forest. Occasionally, we were rewarded with glimpses of the summit. A fair amount of the hike soon consisted of taking zig zag paths up and down small canyons. As we continued these became larger. And larger. And larger. Now our elevation map indeed warned us of "Little Zig Zag Canyon" and

"Big Zig Zag Canyon" but we weren't precisely sure where we were relative to these named canyons.

As we encountered ever larger canyons, we kept revising our idea about where we were. As we finished one canyon, we would always say, "Well, that must have been Big Zig Zag Canyon, so we must be *here* on the map." At one point, after just deciding that we had conquered Big Zig Zag Canyon, we emerged from a grove of hemlock to a gaping maw of the mountain. It completely dwarfed anything we had seen before. Obviously, the much lesser giant we had already conquered was only "Little Zig Zag Canyon" and we were only now truly facing "Big Zig Zag Canyon." It probably took at least an hour to descend and re-ascend. As those of you who have ever climbed on a mountain know, changing elevation is much like traveling in time. As we descended, the cold frozen ground of winter gave way to the first signs of spring.

As we continued our descent, weeds and flowers abounded and trees sported bud and leaf. At the bottom of the ravine, it felt like a summer day. And, again, on the way up, there was the feeling of time travel compression. We were climbing through weeks of season change in minutes. At last we reached the top of the trail and looked back at this canyon which would have been much better named "Gargantuan Zig Zag Canyon"! One last look and we turned back to the path into another forests. At the entrance to the forest, I noticed there was a small wooden sign oriented toward people leaving the forest and entering the canyon. Curious, I ventured back to read the sign: "Little Zig Zag Canyon." What!!?? That enormous *chasm* in the earth was *little* Zig Zag Canyon?

Up to this point, our hike had been vigorous but not dangerous. However, now a small and subtle danger did present itself. We would have to press pretty hard to make it back to the car by dark. We had not bought provisions for an over-night stay. Hiking in the dark is dangerous. And, it gets really cold at night. So, now the question was, could we cross the next canyon and still get back by dark? We decided we could. Clearly, "Big" Zig Zag Canyon was a name chosen in a paroxysm of frolicking understatement while "Little" Zig Zag Canyon was just a bald-faced lie.

Like it or not, all of us now journey on spaceship earth. We are traveling together with everyone else on the planet. We are in a crazy dance of multiple motions spinning, circling, spiraling through the universe at horrific speed. Neither a single person on the planet nor all of us collectively have a guaranteed comprehensive plan for how to avoid any one of a number of ecological disasters. Throughout the planet, there are numerous religions and cultures. Getting along with each other would be critical, even if many countries did not have nuclear weapons, which, in fact, they do. To enhance the adrenaline rush, these various countries and cultures and religions are associated with many different languages and stories about how we got to where we are today. Everyone, in other words, has a different map. There are no posted signs. No-one owns a compass.

I could say, "Fasten Your Seat Belts Folks. We are in for turbulence." I could say that. But that would bend the spaceship metaphor beyond the breaking point. But if we think of ourselves as *passive passengers* on a race car, plane, or space ship that someone else, perhaps even someone competent, like Captain Kirk or even God, is piloting, I believe that stance pretty much guarantees that humanity's days are numbered.

No, I think a more apt metaphor is that we are embarked on a vigorous and potentially dangerous hike. Sometimes, it will feel as though you are going backwards in time and sometimes forward at lightning speed. Everywhere along the path, you will have to watch your step, even as you take the time to appreciate the beauty still surrounding you. And just when you think you have conquered the biggest challenge we have ever faced, a still larger challenge will appear.

We did make it back to our car just as night began swallowing all the heat and all the light. I remain hopeful that humanity can survive its crazy, spinning, galactic hike.

10 THE INVISIBILITY CLOAK OF HABIT

"No, you're not wrong; I'm wrong!"

How often have you heard, or uttered these words? Seldom is my guess. In fact, you may have even misread these words. Look again.

Michigan winters are hard. Even in the lower part of the lower peninsula in Ann Arbor, where I attended grad school, winters are long, snowy, bitterly cold, and often feature treacherous ice storms. That sort of winter made springtime all the more soul-saving. Often, when it was sunny and warm, I would teach my "Intro Psych" classes outside on the lawn near Angel Hall. Nearby ran one of the "main drags" in town including a T-shaped intersection. The side street emptying into the main drag included a stop sign for the first three years I lived in Ann Arbor. And, then, there was a change. Whatever the design rationale, the highway department reversed the situation so that traffic on the main drag now had stop signs both ways and the side street was free to turn onto the main drag. That doesn't seem like a huge change, does it?

Yet, my classes were often interrupted by screeching tires and honking horns. Society had not yet "evolved" to the point of pulling a gun and shooting someone for a traffic *faux pas*. That would still require years of work on the part of the NRA to convince people that they needed "protection" for road rage, which coincidentally made road rage that much more deadly. But back in the 1970's, my classes were not interrupted with gunshots. But aside from the screeching tires and honking horns, we could hear plenty of screamed profanity.

What made that an interesting situation to discuss for my intro psych class was that it was never the people who actually had the right of way who did the honking and screaming. It was always (as far as we observed) the people who sailed right through the new — and unseen — stop signs! These stop signs were in *plain view.* This was not at all like the stop sign I sailed through years later in Westchester County New York. That Westchester stop sign was well-hidden behind trees and then made nearly invisible by the intentional addition of green spray paint. I guess some teen-agers thought it would be pretty cool to cause an auto accident. Sigh. But let's teleport back again through time and space to Ann Arbor a couple decades earlier. Those new Ann Arbor stop signs were large and clearly visible to anyone. In fact, both these oversized signs were easily visible to the psych class from 75 yards away. The signs were apparently under an spell. They were invisible to drivers who had driven the main drag for many years. They "knew" the stop signs were not there. They "knew" there was a stop sign on the cross street. So, to many (not all) drivers, these stops signs were under an "invisibility cloak" created by their own expectations.

Furthermore, when drivers did sail through the stop sign and then found themselves almost in an accident, slamming on their breaks and swerving to avoid the accident with a crossing car, it was invariably followed by a loud blaming exercise. The "blame" of course, was always hurled onto the *other* driver — the one actually following the (revised) signage. In the five or six near misses we observed, we *never* saw someone sail through a stop sign and then realize their mistake and apologize. Nope. Not once. It was always an anger display at the "idiot" who had gone right through the (non-existent) stop sign. If you read the last chapter about "Big Zig Zag Canyon" you are already familiar with how our expectations of reality can be slow to catch up with actual reality.

Such situations remind me a little of tether ball. As a reminder, tether ball is played with a ball that is… tethered. The ball is much like a volleyball but connected by a rope to a pole. The players try to hit the ball and wind it completely around the pole in "their" direction. (This game is made for two righties or two lefties). Anyway, as the cord wraps itself around the pole once, the cord shortens and the radius of the ball path is shorter meaning it comes around more quickly. So you need to adjust your timing. But the typical behavior, at least for beginners, is to jump up a little late because everyone bases their timing on the *previous* cycle rather than the *next* cycle. The player realizes they are late and adjusts their timing. Unfortunately, they typically adjust to the last cycle and are once again late. They do keep adjusting but always one revolution too late. As a result, the ball whips around faster and faster wrapping itself into the pole.

In attempts to build artificial general intelligence (AGI) systems, computer scientists encounter the "update problem." As the world changes, so too, the system must change its reactions. But what kind of change in the environment is related to which changes in necessary reactions? In many cases, humans are pretty good at this; in other cases, not so much. Let's say, for instance, that you routinely set your clock radio for 7 am in the morning. One evening, you go out for dinner at the Fish Market and bring home left-overs which you put in your fridge. Now, you should immediately go and make sure your alarm is still set for 7 am, right? No, of course not! You have a model of the world that enables you to realize without any conscious thought that putting leftovers into the fridge in the kitchen will not change your alarm setting.

Let's take another example. You drive to a golf course and park. You take out your clubs and get ready to play a round. But you realize you need a new golf glove so you buy one at the check-in desk. Fine. But now you play the entire round wondering where your car will be when you're done. No you don't! Of course not! Again, your model of the world allows you to realize that there is no way buying a new golf glove can cause your car to appear in a different place. (This is not in actuality *completely* true. Someone at the check-in desk could look at the credit card you used to buy the glove, ask for ID, realize you are going to be occupied with golf for the next 3-5 hours, call their buddy at the DMV, find out your license plate and then call their car thief buddy who finds your car and steals it. That's extremely unlikely but theoretically possible.)

What is mainly easy for humans is not that easy for AI systems. Such systems could be configured in such a way that whenever *anything* changes, it needs to recheck *everything*. This heuristic, however, would slow even a moderately complex system to a crawl.

Occasionally, people are confused about the update problem as well. As AI becomes more ubiquitously integrated with the Internet of Things, our own models of what is related to what may well be as outmoded as those of the unfortunate Ann Arbor drivers. You believe putting something in your fridge cannot affect your alarm setting. And that is certainly true for your "dumb" fridge. But what about a "smart" fridge? It might infer, based on your past behavior, that you are likely to eat the leftovers for breakfast. Your home command center reads the bar codes on your leftovers and realizes it will take you an extra five minutes to consume the dinner-breakfast you brought home. So, it automatically changes your alarm to 6:55. Helpful? Even today, how many of us can really say for certain what the interactions are among the remote controls and settings for the various components of our home entertainment systems?

Here's an "update" error of my own that I remember. We had a small workout room at NYNEX Science and Technology where I ran the Artificial Intelligence lab. In this small workout room was an ordinary wall clock. For years, I used the workout room around noon, and sometimes I glanced at the clock to check the time. At one point, the exercise equipment was moved around and I realized that the clock would now be much easier to see if it were relocated to the opposite wall. So, I moved it. I got on the treadmill and about ten minutes later glanced at the clock to check the time. Only I did *not glance at the clock*. I glanced at where the clock *used to be*. Think about that. I *myself* had moved the clock a few minutes earlier. Obviously, I "knew" where the clock was now positioned. And yet, I felt like one of those Ann Arbor drivers.

The "invisibility cloak of expectation" also appeared when I worked at the IBM Watson Research Center. Several Nobel Prize winners worked there. Anyway, the computer science department was housed for many years in an office building in Hawthorne, New York. Restrooms were conveniently located near the stairwells on every floor. On three of the four floors, the men's room was on the right. But on one of the floors, the women's room was on the right. Whether the designers did this knowingly for a joke, I am not sure. But on the "odd" floor, men often wandered into the women's room and women into the men's room. Now, the doors for these restrooms were not marked in Kanji characters or ancient Greek. No, they were *clearly* marked in English. Although the computer science department consisted of people from all over the world, they all read English quite well. But expectations apparently trump perception. That seems to be the case for everyone some of the time and for some people nearly all the time regardless of intelligence or education. People very often see (or don't see) based on expectations rather than the evidence of their senses.

Is there anything that can be done to help us remove our blinders and see what is really there? I think so, but it isn't easy. The first line of defense is social. What do other people see? Chances are, if you were milling around in a park and suddenly everyone else starting running and screaming away from the swing set, you probably would too even if you saw nothing at all unusual. However, in the Mysterious Case of the Ann Arbor Stop Sign, people immediately interpreted the other driver's behavior, not as another independent source of information, but as proof that the other person was a careless or demented driver. Not only did the drivers not see the "obvious" stop sign but they completely overlooked the possibility that they might have been wrong themselves.

This may be "human nature" but I suspect that this aspect of human nature is exaggerated in some countries by an overly competitive school system and an overly competitive society. In school, we are molded to strive for good grades. Ideally, "grades" would not be so much about comparing people but about realizing what you still needed to learn. In my society, we have perverted such intrinsically social and cooperative activities as dancing, cooking, singing, and dating into "contests." At work, too often, a project failure results in finger-pointing rather than problem solving and prevention of making similar errors in the future. Whatever the reason, it seems incontrovertible that people in our society are bunny-quick to blame others and tortoise-slow to blame themselves.

In *The Walking People* by Paula Underwood, she describes the "Iroquois Rule of Six." This is a rule of thumb the tribe used in order to avoid over-focusing on the very first explanation of behavior that springs to mind. Suppose you work for a large multi-national IT company and find yourself sitting alone in meeting room. You glance at the clock. It says 10:10. You take out your calendar, whether paper or electronic, and re-read your note: "Meet Joe, 10 am, P-45." Here it is 10:10 and he hasn't shown up! It is natural to have some thought like this trounce through your head:

"What the hell? What's wrong with Joe? I guess he just doesn't care about our project!"

Maybe. But the Iroquois Rule of Six might get you to consider at least five alternatives such as: 1. Maybe Joe is from a culture where 10:15 is "on time" for a 10 am meeting. 2. Maybe you wrote down the wrong room. 3. Maybe you wrote down the wrong time. 4. Maybe you wrote down the wrong date. 5. Maybe you are not actually in P-45. 6. Maybe the clock is wrong. 7. Maybe Joe cares about the project but is stuck in traffic. And so on. It isn't so much that we human beings grab on to the first thing that pops into mind. The problem is that once we *do* grab onto an interpretation of events, we find it devilishly difficult to let go! We don't even like to *consider* other possibilities.

My grade school friend Homer had an uncle who fought in the Pacific Theater in WWII. He gave Homer this really cool book about how to survive off the land. One thing I read in that book stuck with me. Monkeys are among the *easiest* wild animals to catch, not because they are *stupid* but because they are *smart*. One simple technique is to put two holes in a coconut shell and hollow it out as much as possible. Then, you slip a treat like a nut or small piece of fruit inside. The monkey comes along and grabs hold of the treat. Their hand, which went easily into the hole cannot get out while their fists are balled up holding the treat. So, you walk up to the monkey and club it and cook it and eat it. Monkeys are fast. It would be easy for the monkey to let go of the treat and scamper away. But they won't. (At least, that is what the manual claimed). How much are we like the monkey? We grab at an explanation that makes us feel good and stick with it. We cannot let go. And we cannot accept the possibility that we ourselves might be wrong. Only in that last split second before the monkey's skull is split open does it perhaps think, "Let go. Run. Too late." Can we humans do better?

The United States, among other countries, has the intellectual capacity and the urgent need to quickly and fully develop new energy sources that are cheap, reliable, renewable, clean, and not dependent on foreign wars. And we are. In a trickle. But we are giving corporate welfare to old energy oil company kingpins because they are lavish campaign donors with a torrential river of cash. If you had a huge hole in your pocket that was draining all your cash, you'd see to fixing it quickly. But the oil drain isn't so obvious. It steals far more of your money than a pickpocket could or a holey pair of jeans. But our tax gifts to oil barons have been well-hidden. Such gifts might even have once been a good idea. Furthermore, at least until lately, oil money doesn't come right out and say, "We know we're rich but we deserve it. We deserve it because we're *great*. And you know we're great because we're *rich*. Give us more!" But we are so much in the habit of using non-renewable resources that we don't think twice about it. Those habits and expectations are played upon so that many are trained to think: "EPA-who needs it?" "Climate Change - unproven science", "Solar and wind power are great but way off in the future", "Pollution may cause cancer and asthma but that's the price of civilization."

The cheap oil prize that we so greedily grabbed hold of is now the trap that will get us killed, quite literally. It's what we've been holding onto for many years. Why let go now? Instead, it's easier to scream at others: "There is no stop sign here!!" Eventually of course, people change and civilizations change. To change too slowly means you could be the cause of an accident; you glance on the wrong wall to see the time; you miss the tether ball on every cycle. Or, it could just mean the complete annihilation of humanity. Maybe you could at least let go for a little while. Maybe you could at least let go with one hand. Maybe you could just forget the prize and the coconut and get away before it's too late. I hope so.

I work to remain hopeful.

11 CITY MOUSE AND COUNTRY MOUSE

I first heard the story of the city mouse and country mouse around four years of age. Briefly, the city mouse invites his cousin, country mouse, to visit him in the city. At first, the country mouse is quite impressed with the array of food available in the city mouse's home. Then, the house cat springs toward them with its sharp claws and long pointed teeth and nearly rips the mice apart. In the end, the country mouse scampers back and shouts back to his city cousin something to the effect that he's happy to have his bread crumbs in peace rather than risking life and limb in the city. The exact words, I don't recall, but they have probably suffered in the translation from Aesop's ancient Greek to modern English and even more severely in the translation from mouse-speak to human speech. Most likely, the original sounded something like this: "Squeak. Squeak! Squeak."

No doubt, living in either the city or the country provides a mouse with various advantages and disadvantages. Both places have sources of food and both have predators. But what about human beings? Here too, there are advantages and disadvantages of living in a large city versus living in the country or a small town. While human beings undoubtedly have many behaviors that are influenced by "instinct," people's behavior is often even more influenced by learning than by instinct. Moreover, because we humans can talk and write and are fundamentally social beings, not only do urban and rural environments result in different kinds of *individual* skills, in a fairly short time, they also result in different *cultures*.

These differences are not arbitrary but are adaptations to the characteristics of urban and rural environments.

In cities (and especially coastal cities), people typically come in contact with a huge variety of people. Many metropolitan areas feature different cuisines, attractions, races, religions, sexual preferences, and so on. Take the matter of cuisine. It is easy in New York City, San Francisco, Atlanta, Boston, Washington DC, Seattle, Minneapolis, Los Angeles, or San Diego to find restaurants that serve excellent Italian, French, Japanese, Chinese, Mexican, Vegetarian, Vegan, Ethiopian, Jewish or Indian food. I happen to love them all! But for someone who hates any of these options, it is also easy to avoid such cuisine. You don't care for Indian food? No problem. Don't go. Suppose however, you are with a group of friends and everyone else wants to go for sushi which you happen to hate. The vast majority of urban Japanese restaurants in the USA offer other options that are "close to" traditional American cuisine. So, you can go to a Japanese restaurant with your friends and order steak teriyaki while they all eat raw fish.

But let's just suppose that for whatever reason, you are *so* appalled by raw fish that you get sick merely by watching someone else eating it. Well, you simply don't watch. Now, the thing about living in a big city is that you don't have to create this solution on your own. That's what everyone does. If they see something they don't like, they look away. They learn not to dwell on it. It's very crowded in a city. If you walk around or take public transportation and are "offended" or "put off" by anyone who speaks differently, dresses differently, eats differently, worships differently, looks different, etc. you are going to quickly become completely stressed out and become one completely unhappy camper.

People in large cities instead learn to be polite and focus their energy on the places and people that *do* give them joy. It takes time to find friends but eventually you find people who share fundamental interests and values. They might be next door, but more likely, they are are a subway ride or a long walk away. There are literally more than a million people in any large city that you never get to know. But because there are so many choices, many opportunities arise to do what you like and many friends will join you. You might love tennis, roller skating, and art museums. You might never step foot in the science museum or the public library or the parks. It's all fine. The culture of the city is tolerance for everyone.

Yet, people select those they get to know from a huge pool. If you come from, say, China, and you want to stick with other Chinese people, you can easily do that. You can survive in New York City or San Francisco without having to experience Mexican food or even without learning much English. On the other hand, if you want to become assimilated into more "mainstream" American culture and eat pizza every day and listen to jazz and dress like a Native America — hey, you're welcome to do that too. Because everyone passes by people that are so different every day, almost everyone learns tolerance. In essence, you see, there is not "one" New York City or Los Angeles, there are thousands! People essentially live in their own version of these cities and become close only with a small group of like-minded people. Of course, your "tennis friends" might be different from your "roller skating friends" which might be a slightly different group than your "art museum friends." But even putting all your friends together, the people you know are only 1/10,000 or 1/100,000 of the people in the city. You essentially have many of the pleasures of a small town in that "virtual town" - your own circle of friends.

One downside of big city living is that you may never get to know your next door neighbors. You and they may simply have very different tastes and interests. Besides that, there is a lot of turnover in a city. Often, there doesn't seem to be much point in becoming friends simply because you live next door. Partly, this is because they (or you) are quite likely to move away in a month.

There is a worse down side to big cities. At the extreme, the distance that people create mentally to accommodate the extremely close physical proximity and the culture of leaving others alone also makes it possible for someone to be stabbed on the street without anyone helping. This phenomenon has been studied and is called "bystander behavior." People may actually be much more likely to help if they are the *only* witness than if they are one of 100. Each of the 100 looks around and sees that none of the other 99 are doing anything and so conclude, all evidence to the contrary, that nothing much is happening or else the other 99 people would be helping. (You can see more detail on the likelihood that the bystander effect would be less in a small town than in a big city in Wikipedia: Cohesiveness and group membership).

In any case, the "culture" that arises in cities is typically quite tolerant of differences, somewhat distant from the vast majority of your fellow citizens but certainly allows for close friendships based on any combination of a hundred different factors. Because large cities develop a culture of tolerance for other types of people, that fact becomes known and attracts still more diversity which in turn encourages more tolerance and diversity.

There is another important aspect of living in a large city. It is crowded and complex. You constantly have to "trust" people you don't know: those who drive the taxis, deliver the food, come to fix your cable, police the streets and so on. These are typically not people you know. In fact, for the most part, you won't ever see them again. But it is impractical not to trust all these strangers. Most of the time, the trust works out though on rare occasions, it backfires.

The experience of living in a small rural town is completely different. There are not 400 different restaurants to choose from. There might be three. Possibly one of the three is ethnic, but it is not likely. A Korean restaurant in New York City can be quite profitable if only .01% of the NYC population goes there regularly. That won't work in Woburn MA or Bend OR though, let alone in a town of 5000. A small town in America may well have a baseball diamond and a public library. But they are unlikely to have a holography museum or a laser tag facility. The modest number of people living in a small town means, in essence, that the citizens must agree on what types of restaurants are available, what recreational facilities are available, what clothing stores are in town and so on.

In addition, everyone in town is likely to run into everyone else again and again. Rather than learning to avoid and look away and ignore things you don't personally care for, people in small towns instead lean in. They want to know what exactly is going on with everyone else in town. Everyone soon knows who the town drunk is and who is having an affair with whom. People in small towns do not typically think, "It's none of my business" but that's exactly what people in large cities think.

For these reasons, people in small towns are less likely to learn the skill of looking away. If they personally hate sushi and end up visiting their cousin in a big city like Chicago and then end up in a Japanese restaurant, they are both fascinated and disgusted by watching their cousin eat sushi. They could *theoretically* just look away, but that is not a very well learned skill for most who have only lived in small towns. For this reasons, the culture of the small town also evolves to be different from that of a large city. People in small towns who thrive on diversity, who are themselves different, or who believe strongly in tolerance feel as though they don't belong. They also feel deprived of interesting possibilities, so most end up moving away. Of course, that makes the town even more homogeneous. The small town ends up being *much* more "tight knit" than a random group of 5000 people in a large city. It seems much less likely people would fail to help someone being stabbed on the street.

In a small town, since people know almost everyone they interact with, they don't really have to trust strangers all that much. If someone new delivers the mail, the small town person is likely to ask whether they just moved into town, where they came from and exactly where they now live and so on. This would be considered rude and even weird in a big city. People in a small town probe to know people in their small town. They tune *in* not *out*. They are much more likely to choose friends partly on the basis of location rather than vocation. Because of this cluster of factors, people in one small town are more likely to stay in that small town. It is probably much more "disruptive" to move from Woburn MA to Bend OR than to move from New York City to Los Angeles. Of course, either move means you will have to learn where things are, get a new driver's license, make new friends etc., but the "culture" of cities is becoming similar all across America and indeed, all across the world. Two small towns can have quite different cultures.

People in a small town are likely to know the police whom they come in contact with. If a police officer in a small town arrests someone or even shoots them, people in a small town are much more likely to know both the police officer and the person arrested (or shot). Provided the police officer is generally known to be fair-minded person, the people in the small town are much more likely to be sympathetic. In addition, it may well known that the person arrested (or even shot) is and has been a "bad guy" the whole time he's been in town.

In a large city, by contrast, people who read or hear about someone making an arrest are unlikely to know personally either the policeman or the suspect. They probably still have a presumption that the police probably acted correctly. However, their reactions are much more likely to vary from person to person than what you would find in a small town.

Cities do differ from each other in terms of culture, yet small towns may differ even more. For example, Murray Hill, New Jersey is not a huge city (population around 3500). However, many of the people living there worked at Bell Labs, a large famous research institute long part of AT&T but now part of Nokia. That particular small area includes residents from many countries, liberal and very well funded schools, and so on. Small towns that grow up around trade centers, farming communities, research centers and universities, or coal mining undoubtedly have very different typical "cultures." Similarly, a large city like New York that has people from all over the world is quite different than one of the Chinese cities around large-scale manufacturing facilities (e.g., Guangzhou or Shenzhen). In other cases, a town's citizens might have largely migrated from another country and brought some of that culture with them.

What can small town cultures and big city cultures learn from each other? How can these cultures tolerate each other? Is there a way to have the advantages of both? If humanity keeps exponentially increasing its population, will there even be any "small towns" left in 100 or 500 years? That's up to the collective will of humanity.

12 MATH CLASS: WHO ARE YOU?

Rest assured, the "math" in this chapter does not require integral calculus, differential equations, trigonometry, or even algebra. In fact, if you prefer, you can call the chapter "Christianity" or "Buddhism" because you would reach the same conclusions even from one of those very different pathways.

Part of the inspiration for this chapter came from visiting the Smithsonian Institute about 20 years ago. They displayed a large graph with the population of the earth plotted against the year. I looked at my birth year and could easily see that more than half the total earth's population came after my birth year. And, that was 20 years ago. In other words, I am one of the "ancient ones"! More than half the people born since the dawn of civilization were born after I was!

Another inspiration comes from a question I often heard as leader of the artificial intelligence lab at NYNEX. I worked for an ex-Bell Labs engineer, Ed Thomas. People were always asking me whether we were "related." I found this question extremely amusing. Why? Because *we are all related!* In fact, we share about 40% of our genes with *crayfish* and 90% with *horses.* We're closely related to chimps and bonobos though we did not "descend" directly from apes. Yet, in our society, we chose to "draw the line" between being "related" and "not related" way over at one end of the scale. Ed Thomas and I only share about 99.9% of our genes so we are called "unrelated" while my brother and I share 99.95% and so we are (closely) related. Most people would say they are "unrelated" to a horse even though they share 90% of their genes. Weird.

A few days ago, I read that new fossils indicate life on earth is at least 4.75 billion years old. When I was a kid, starting around age 7, I became (like many others) fascinated by dinosaurs. At that point, the best guesses were that life was somewhere between 500 million years old and 1 billion years old. In the course of my lifetime, that estimate more than quadrupled.

Who cares and why does all this matter? Apart from curiosity, it matters because it allows us to put in perspective our own individual lives in the context of life on planet earth.

Most people, most of the time, love their children and generally put the welfare of their kids even above their own. This is how life progresses. So far as we know, individuals never live forever, at least in this physical world. However, life as a whole continues to live and our direct descendants and relatives continue to live after our death. So, how much of "your" genetic material is actually in *you* versus how much is in all your cousins?

To simplify, let's start with just other human beings. There are currently (2018) about 7 billion people on the planet. You are one of them. You share 99.9% of your genes with those folks.

So, let's see. There's you. And you have 7 billion relatives. A few are slightly more related than 99.9% identical genes, but let's just say 99.9%. That means the total genome of your genes is in one person (you) who has 100% of your genes and 7 billion others who "only" have 99.9% of your genes. 99.9% of 7 billion is 6,993,000,000 while 100% of 1 is (by my reckoning) 1.000. In other words, the total amount of "your" genes that is in other people is 6,993,000,000 as much as lies within the physical boundaries of your own skin. Not an equal amount. Not 10x as much. Not 100x as much. Not even a million times as much. No. Nearly *seven billion times as much.*

From the standpoint of genes, this vastly *understates* the case because there are 7-10 million species on earth besides humans. All of these share some of your genes and many of them share a lot of your genes. Of course, we humans are relatively big and while there are some plants and animals much bigger than we are, there is more mass of life in bacteria than blue whales or redwoods. In principle, one can calculate a better number by taking into account, for each of 7-10 million species how many cells are in each; how populous they are, and what percentage of genes are in common between humans (and therefore you) and each of these species. It's straightforward but tedious. I gave up after 100,000 species. No, I didn't. I never started because I knew I would give up way before I got to 100,000. In many cases, we don't even have a very good estimate of the populations. Given all the trees, grasses, bacteria, insects, fish, plankton, etc. I would guesstimate that adding all the genes in all the other plants and animals would mean the genes in your body represent at most about one in a trillion of all the copies of those genes on earth. So, from the standpoint of ensuring the propagation of your genes, caring about your own physical life represents about 1/1000000000000 of the total.

I grant you that genes are not all that matters in human life. And, I want to explore some of the other aspects of the interconnectedness of life apart from a common genetic heritage. However, first, it is really worth taking a moment to let that fraction sink in.

It isn't as though the "you" inside your skin weighs, say, 150 pounds while the "you" that is outside your skin is, say, the size of a blue whale. No. In fact, even 1000 blue whales compared with your physical body is not so lop-sided a comparison. To gain some perspective on the enormous fraction of your genes that is *not* inside your skin, imagine thirty galactic clusters of stars. Each of those thirty clusters has 100 stars. Each of those stars has 10 planets to support life. Each of those planets has 100 oceans and each of those oceans has 1000 blue whales. Versus you.

Another way to think about is that when you physically die, it is a little like "trimming" or "pruning" the "Tree of Life." But your dying would not be like cutting off a branch. Or a twig. Or a leaf. It would be like shaving an invisible razor thin strip off one needle of one twig of one branch of a huge Redwood.

It is understood that life is partly (yet by no means wholly) about competition. Each and every one of those bits of "you" that is in other life-forms is not necessarily your best buddy. You may share a lot of DNA with a great white shark but you still might not wish him well.

Or, you might not much like your cousins the mosquitoes and deer flies and pneumonia germs. The problem is that we are not collectively anywhere near to being smart enough to understand the effects of deleting certain species and not others. (Personally, I would be very tempted to destroy all the mosquitos and deer flies). Perhaps, some day in a hundred years or so, we might understand enough to intelligently redesign an ecosystem. Don't hold your breath though. Despite the fact that some of those individual species and some individuals within a species are annoying, we really have no idea how to extract some one thing. It is not a set of legos. Every species is connected with a variety of chemical and mechanical connections to hundreds of others. It is more like trying to extract your iPhone adapter from your backpack which also contains headphones, power cords, adapters for five other devices and, for good measure, a couple of stray shoelaces.

You could also point out, quite rightly, that not all genes are as "fundamental" to making you you as are other genes. There are genes, perhaps, that make your eyes blue or brown. Does that seem fundamental to your uniqueness? Or, perhaps there's a gene that determines whether the design of your thumbprint is a whorl or loop. Does that seem fundamental to who you are and to your life? On the other hand, there are genes that make you want to live and find love and raise a family and contribute and play and learn. To me, those are the genes that are fundamental and guess what? Those are the very genes that you *share* with millions of other species. Naturally, we humans like to think of ourselves as fundamentally different from other species on the planet

and in some ways we are. As discussed below, being able
to communicate so many messages with other people
across time and space and even after death indeed makes
people "different" but when it comes to the things you
are likely to care the *most* about: staying alive, avoiding
pain, keeping your family healthy, fighting off disease —
those are pretty common across animals and even plants
and bacteria, at least in rudimentary form. Just because
an ant doesn't do calculus doesn't mean it doesn't work
to stay alive and help it's colony do the same. The
Internet abounds with videos that should convince you
how similar mammals are to each other and to us.

Speaking of math classes, let us turn to some of the other
aspects of how our own individual life fits with the larger
web of life. Consider learning. Pretty much all life is able
to learn. Humans, however, are able to communicate
through speech, writing, and pictures. This means that we
can learn across continents and generations.
Communication affects behavior. Everyone is exposed to
unique information so that people also end up acting very
differently and even perceiving things differently. So,
when it comes to human beings, many of the differences
we think important are in the ideas and attitudes people
have as well as their actual behavioral differences. To put
it simplistically, we largely feel akin to others on the
basis of how we think and feel, not just on the proportion
of genes we share. Many of the labels that we put on
people — in fact, the vast majority of them — focus on
these sorts of differences. For example, we have:
extrovert, introvert, flirt, workaholic, physicist,
physician, psychologist, psychic, psycho, Republican,
Democrat, liberal, heterosexual, homosexual, creative,

drudge, etc. But what part of what people actually do is different? How much is the same? How *fundamental* are the differences in behaviors and ideas?

What proportion of all human knowledge do we have in our own brain? How fundamental is that personal knowledge? Humans have used spoken language for, let us say, 100,000 years. People can learn about four "chunks" per second. A "chunk" is basically a new configuration of things you already know. We measure the information in a computer in terms of "bits" but this turns out not to be a very good measure for people (or other animals). If you have to learn "A CAD" (a bad man) it is pretty easy. It is essentially only one "chunk." If you know how to read hexadecimal then "ACAD" is equal to 10-12-10-13. It is easier to remember "ACAD" than to remember "10-12-10-13." That in turn is easier than the binary string: "1010110010101101" though they have the same number of bits. In the same way, it is much easier to recall the password: "Thistooshallpass" than the password: "ooassllapsTsthih." That is the basic concept behind "chunks" as a measure. How easily we learn new things depends heavily on what we already know. One major problem with trying to learn a new language is that we keep thinking of it (and even *hearing* it) in terms of the language we already know. In fact, studies with infants show that by a few *weeks* of age, they are already *less* able than they were at birth to distinguish sounds that make no meaningful difference in their native language.

Psychology is endlessly fascinating! But let's return to our calculations. If you are awake, on average for 16 hours a day for your lifetime of 100 years, you would have an opportunity to learn 4 chunks/second x 60 seconds/minute x 60 minutes/hour x 16 hours/day x 365 days/year x 100 years for a total of 12,600,000,000 chunks! That is a lot! Of course, that is rather an ideal case. If you watch the same TV shows and hang out with the same people you may not get your full allotment of 12 billion chunks worth of learning, but it's still going to be a lot.

People have been communicating and learning through speech for at least 100,000 years. That is more than 1000 times as long as you've been alive. For a long time, the population of the earth was far less than today, but let's say there were about a million people for most of that time. Since each person grows up in a different environment, they learn different things. Leaving aside the fact that the population of the earth is now about 7 billion and just using the very conservative 1 million figure, you know about 1/1000000000 or a *billionth* of what humans collectively have learned. (For a more in-depth estimate, check out the link below).

http://www.livescience.com/54094-how-big-is-the-internet.html

A more direct way to think about this is that collectively today, on average, you know about 1/7000000000 of the knowledge of humanity since you are only one person and there are seven billion on the planet. If you've been learning for about 70 years (as I have) then you may know a slightly higher fraction of the total knowledge. Let's just take the conservative estimate that your knowledge is one billionth. But how much is a billion? It's hard to visualize.

One way to think about it is the following metaphor. You, as an individual, have one "book" of knowledge in your head. (It's a rather large one, but all of the books in this example will also be rather large). Now, let's consider that the whole world of knowledge exists on ten continents. Each continent has 25 countries for a total of 250 countries. Each of these countries has 40 cities. Each of these cities has 10 libraries. Each of these libraries has 10 rooms and each room has 1000 books each of which is every bit as complete and weighty as your own.

Much of your knowledge is common, but a lot of it is unique. No-one has lived the life you have and so your "book" will contain a lot that is about your own experience. And that's true as well for each of the other 7 billion people on earth. So, while the biological stuff that makes you you, is hugely outside your own skin, it's also true that the knowledge in your own skull is but a teeny fraction of what humanity has collectively learned. Best to share what you know before you die; afterwards, it will be inaccessible to others. Aside from that sage advice, you might reflect that indeed, *none of us* knows very much at all compared with what we *collectively* know *as a species*.

The other major way that we interact with each other and with every living thing on the planet is through our chemical exchanges. People, such as you and me, for example, inhale air that contains oxygen. We cannot live without it. Where does the oxygen come from? Green plants. To many people, "tree hugger" is a slam, an insult, a term that is meant to be demeaning. Okay, I grant you, actually hugging a tree is probably something that doesn't mean much to the tree. However, without green plants and the oxygen they produce, people (and other animals) would die off. Not only do plants produce oxygen but they also get rid of carbon dioxide. Of course, without green plants, there would be few foods from plants and we would have to "eat" mostly animals for the short time the supply lasted. A lack of green plants would really have four ways to end humanity: greatly increased carbon dioxide causing global warming, lack of sufficient food, lack of sufficient oxygen, too much carbon dioxide to survive. Probably, the lack of food would do us in first. You could actually hug much worse things than trees.

In any case, the oxygen - carbon dioxide and food cycles are two of the important ways that we are chemically interconnected with the entire web of life on the planet. Another important cycle is the nitrogen cycle. While plants are ultimately at the root of what we eat, the bodies of humans and other animals eventually provide important nitrogen for plants. Most plants are quite patient about waiting passively for us to die before partaking of our bodies. But there are some much pluckier plants such as the pitcher plant, sundew, and Venus flytrap which actually trap animals such as insects and small frogs in order to "feed" on them to supply the plant's nitrogen needs.

These cycles have been going on for a very long time. The new thing that humans bring to the party is sadly not a nice cabernet or chardonnay, but rather a *toxic cocktail of chemicals that never existed before.* Some of these are intentionally produced to be lethal and others are bad side-effects of useful things. But rest assured, these "new" chemicals are overwhelmingly bad for nearly everything in the biosphere. They are bad for you, for your kids, for your grandchildren, for frogs, redwoods, and honeybees. They are bad for almost everybody and every species. For instance, you may find it convenient to buy "air fresheners." These do not actually "freshen" the air. They have three important classes of chemicals: something that screws up your hormones; something that is a known carcinogen; something that destroys your sense of smell. "Air freshener" indeed. (Check them out in toxipedia!).

It strikes me as odd that adults in many parts of the world are "not allowed" to buy "street drugs" while any seven year old can walk in to a grocery and buy an "air freshener" which could cause numerous problems. The other issue is that even though you exercise your freedom to buy your air freshener, eventually those chemicals in "your" air freshener end up in *my* lungs and the lungs of my descendants as well as the lungs of monkeys, parrots and rabbits. The polluting chemicals eventually end up pretty well scattered throughout the world. China's air pollution eventually gets to Americans and American air pollution gets to China. This is not just a contemporaneous phenomenon. Calculations show that we all have inhaled air molecules that were exhaled from everyone who has ever lived on earth!

To make an overly long story short, we are all highly interconnected and most of what makes you, *you* is not inside the confines of your own body. For me, this puts unfettered greed in the category of being just plain silly. Who do you think you are? If you think it's worth it to destroy the entire tree of life to satisfy your whims, you are not doing it out of selfishness. Sorry, but you are doing it out of *stupidity.* Because what makes you "you" — the real essence of you genetically, ideologically, and chemically is overwhelmingly not *in* you at all! It is in the biosphere you inhabit. What doth it profit you if you save your own skin at the cost of harming the biosphere? Nothing. No profit. None. It is instead a loss beyond comprehension. We all need to wise up.

13 THE GREAT RACE TO THE FINISH

I really wondered how that whitish-green hard puffy leaf worked. What was it made of? How hard would it be to burst it? And when I did, what would come out? At the age of four, ooze, jelly, a million tiny red spiders, or an emerald all seemed about equally likely. I began to squeeze it with my fingernail, slowly and carefully increasing the pressure. I concentrated so hard I didn't notice my grandpa coming up behind me. He ordered me not to hurt the plant. I asked him to clarify that statement. (Of course, I didn't use precisely those words but I knew the word "hurt" could mean "damage" or "cause pain.") He insisted it was both. I remained skeptical. I knew he took great care of his plants (in this case, I would now guess a defenseless jade plant) so I didn't molest them again.

On the other hand, I never had the slightest doubt that other animals feel pain much as we do. For that matter, I still don't have any doubts. We co-evolved for billions of years and then much more recently differentiated into species such as human, dog, cat, horse. To me, it is much more reasonable to believe emotions and consciousness are in all living things to some degree and in vertebrates to much the same degree as in humans — than to imagine that emotions and consciousness "emerged" when our brains passed some critical threshold of complexity; a theory whose main benefit, it seems to me, has *nothing* to do with parsimony and *everything* to do with a childish excuse to maim or kill anything as it pleases us.

So even at an early age, I at least credited all living animals with being pretty much like us. That is why it shocked me to read in a Walt Disney comic (of all places!) about lemmings following each other over a cliff to drown in the ocean! Why would they do that? Can't they see there's a cliff there? Are the ones in front doing it on purpose? I could imagine some of them get pushed by the ones behind, but what about the last rank? At least they should be scraping their tiny claws into the earth in a last ditch attempt to save their lives. And, if all the lemmings drowned in the sea, how could there be any lemmings left alive?

Only a few short months later, this time in school, I was shocked to learn that buffalo did the same thing! Buffalo! Big headed buffalo. What were they thinking? "Hey, everybody! We wouldn't be stampeding if we weren't headed to the lushest, greenest, tastiest pastures of plenty our herd has ever seen!" And then, in that last second before the terrible and explosive rib smashing landing do they think in their bisonic code equivalent, "Damn!" or "What the…?" or "Oops!" or "Take me, God!" Perhaps it's more likely they were thinking, in essence, "Hey, everybody wouldn't be stampeding unless we were being chased by a horrendous bison-eating monster!" I doubt they think something like, "Whoopee! A stampede! Great chance for me to work a few pounds off. I don't mean to be putting it on, but the grass here is like, so good, man. I eat one blade and the next thing I know, I've munched down the whole patch!"

Of course, from our perspective outside the herd, it looks as though all the lemmings or bison or beached whales agree that their self-destructive behavior is a great idea. It might well be that one, or two, or even many of the bison are just as bewildered as we would be. They might be thinking, "Hold on. Why is everybody rushing so madly toward…what is it exactly? Shouldn't a couple of us go up a hill and see where we're heading? Hello! Let me take a minute…hey! Quit shoving! I'm trying to get a better look! I'm not sure this is…Arghhhh….I knew it!" They are wondering whether a stampede is wise but they are so pressed by the others on all sides, they can't convince the herd to slow down. It is even possible that someone in the herd actually *knows* they are headed for doom and they *still* can't do anything. "Wait, guys! I recognize this patch of sweet clover! We're headed for the cliff! Stop! Stop!" Over they go along with everyone else.

These were serious questions for me as a young child. *I* certainly wanted to live. And, from everything I could tell in life or on the radio or on TV or in the movies or in cartoons or books, *every* living thing wanted to stay alive. But somehow, these creatures were doing something that caused their own deaths! That just seemed perverted. Odd. Weird. Life should be propagating life, not destroying itself. I didn't even need a Bible lesson on that one.

Although I thought animals feel emotions and are conscious, I doubted, even as a child, that they think in words in the way humans do or that they communicate with all the subtlety that we do (despite all those Disney movies). So, it came as yet another shock to learn that sometimes *people* commit suicide. Still later, I learned that they sometimes do it *en masse*! (Google, for instance, the "Heaven's Gate" cult).

Meanwhile, even more commonly, huge numbers of people march off to wars. Many are maimed or killed. In this case, people are generally convinced that they are doing something for their group, tribe, or country. For instance, with two armies lined up at the border, it is pretty much assumed, with some justification, that simply giving up will also result in death or slavery. This kind of destructive behavior is not unique to humans. At about the age I was learning about suicide, my cousin Bob and I observed an ant war between red and black ants in my grandfather's garden. At that point, I already knew about human wars, at least in broad outline, but watching ants fight made it seem perhaps more inevitable that humans too had to fight rather than that they *chose* to fight.

It often seems that soldiers, and indeed, whole nations, are more or less tricked or stampeded into fighting. In that sense, it is effectively a kind of mass suicide but with a lottery system thrown in. Not everyone who fights dies, but there is a real chance of getting maimed or killed. From the perspective of those fighting, it is a brave thing to do — a selfless act that is designed to help save their people and their nation. After the fact, looking back, it sometimes seems that only a few people; e.g., arms dealers and politicians, actually benefit much from wars. For example, Hitler convinced people in Germany that aggression and conquest would be to their benefit and in the newsreels from that time, the masses of people saluting him look every bit as mindless as lemmings following each other over a cliff to drown in the ocean.

On the one hand, humanity devotes a large proportion of their resources to fighting each other, committing crimes, defending against crimes, punishing crimes, defending against invaders, and building machines to help us in fighting other humans. These conflicts always cause massive suffering and always benefit only a few people. Occasionally, these efforts might help reach some national objective that benefits a larger proportion of people. Meanwhile, humanity is collectively headed for numerous cliffs. Although population growth may be slowing, we remain in danger of reproducing way beyond the earth's carrying capacity in terms of food and drinkable water.

At the same time, our activities are contributing to global climate change and to pollution. As our population density increases, and as our immune systems are assaulted with an ever greater quantity and variety of chemicals that make it harder to fight off disease, we face increased odds of a pandemic. And, we are not spending nearly enough money to prevent it.

And, the threat of atomic war still looms. If you were an alien life form visiting earth for the first time from some other solar system, would you not be flabbergasted to learn that we humans have weapons of mass destruction aimed at *each other?*[2] Really? Does anyone really hate a *million* other human beings? Do you hate them enough to incinerate them? Do you even *know* a million human beings in a foreign country? Or, have you convinced

---

[2] See Niven and Pournelle's *Footfall* (1985) for a fascinating story on this theme.

yourself it's okay to kill them because they like weird food or listen to strange music or have different customs, holidays or Gods? Or, perhaps you have been convinced by the most evil politicians on the planet that those people are out to *get you and the people you love.* You might want to check that out first hand.

We can disagree, argue, do more research on *which* cliff we are headed for first, but I want to know this: Why the hell are we headed toward *any* cliff? Why don't we simply decide collectively that we are better than that; that we don't have to plummet off any cliff at all. We can just decide that we need to make this planet habitable for a long long time and collectively decide how to do it. It's a non-trivial exercise, but so is sending people to the moon and building a tunnel under the English Channel. We would not only save the lives of countless people in future generations but also the lives of many of our fellow living beings today.

Or, we could wait until we are over the cliff in free fall. As the ground looms up to us faster and faster, just before we smash to smithereens, we could think to ourselves, "Oh, darn, we should have…"

But we are not lemmings after all, nor bison. We are human beings who are capable of seeing where we are going and changing direction. Right? *Right?*

14 RIPPLES

"Water, water, everywhere nor any drop to drink."

(*The Rhyme of the Ancient Mariner,* Samuel Taylor Coleridge).

One of my earliest memories: splashing water. I know it is an early recollection because of the decontextualized nature of the memory and the lack of color constancy. Let me explain. I recall that yesterday I met with some friends for dinner at True Food Kitchen. I know how I got there. I know why I went there. I know what I had for dinner. We met the manager. We had a great conversation and so on. I know we stopped on the way back to visit my mother-in-law. In other words, any *particular* memory of the sights, smells, tastes, and so on of that evening has been stored in a temporal and spatial context. Granted, this is a much more recent memory, but this kind of contextualization is generally present in my memories after starting school. I recall falling down the steps in first grade. I know why I was at school, where the steps were, that someone pushed me, and so on. But my memory of splashing is simply splashing. In my memory, it is not even splashing really so much as "painting" (in effect) with the water. As an adult, if I recall splashing in the water, I would know where I was, whom I was splashing and so on. I also see the water in the swimming pool I frequented as a teenager as being blue. Of course, reflections on the water would appear as different colors depending on what was nearby. I recall "chicken fights" in which we teenage boys would put girls on our shoulders and each team would try to get the other team to fall apart. It was a fun game that required balance and strength for us "horses" below, and complete body strength and balance for the "rider" above, but, needless to say, the main thrill for a young teen boy was being that close to a girl!

That much earlier vision of splashing though is one of causing the water to appear in patterns and colors by smashing my hands into the water. I was, in effect, conducting an orchestra of color, shape, and noise. Later, there were other adventures in water such as dropping a stone in and watching the ripples go out to the sides of a sink, tub, bucket or pond and watching them reflect off the edges. On and on the ripples went.

I conducted other, larger scale childhood experiments. For example, in the bathtub, I discovered that if I swayed my body in time to my own waves, I could make the waves go higher and higher with each body swing eventually causing the water to reach and then breach the edge of the tub and slosh out onto the floor. Amazing! Making these "tidal waves" did not require great strength. The timing was critical though. I could "stop" the waves by going out of synch. Or, I could make them larger and larger by careful timing. These "ripples" were no longer passive. Adding energy at the right time grew them ever larger. Then, when the water inevitably slopped out onto the floor and seeped through the floor, it caused another kind of "ripple."

Those ripples might be called "behavioral ripples." As a young child, I was concerned with the *vital* and *fundamental* work of trying to understand the basic physical phenomena of the universe. My parents, meanwhile, showed themselves to be far more concerned with *trivial* concerns such as the structural and aesthetic integrity of our house. They made these priorities quite clear. Alas, after a few overflows, my tub experiments had to be limited to creating waves that went *up to* the edge of the tub — but not beyond.

Rain-soaked storm gutters provided a similar challenge. All the kids in my neighborhood wanted to find the deepest possible streams that would pool water up to the very top edge of our black rubber four-buckled boots. Naturally, there is a fine line, often crossed, between water coming up to the very edge of the boot tops and going ever so slightly over the edge. Once the water started going over the edge, however, that water seemed to invite more water to follow along. This foot soaking provided more "behavioral ripples;" namely, finding a way to sneak into the house and not have Mom notice that my shoes, socks, and feet were soaked. Sometimes I succeeded…but most times, I failed. Looking back, it does seem I found water to be a much less "invasive" substance than did my parents. I probably should have been more careful. On the other hand, even looking back, it seems they really exaggerated the damage done to socks, shoes, feet, and floors by a few drops of water. It seems almost as though they were afraid *any* amount of unwanted water in the house could slide down some slippery slope toward flooding or having our house carried away like a little stick raft on a creek. Perhaps having even just a *little* water in the house would invite more and more and soon a *hurricane* might flood the entire neighborhood? I would certainly have agreed with my parents, had they asked, that we should do a lot to prevent a hurricane from ruining our house and all our possessions.

Water fascinates people around the world, not only because it is essential for life, but also because of its strange properties. As a liquid, we all become familiar with its cohesion, waves, and ripples. We marvel at its power to destroy as well as to build. Beyond that, we learn that it changes state. Ice is frozen water. Ice itself exists in many forms such as snowflakes, icebergs, the solid ice of frozen winter ponds, the deceptive nature of candle ice. (As it turns out, under laboratory conditions of extreme pressure, ice can exist in scores of additional crystalline structures). But even in our natural lives, most of us see liquid water and frozen water quite often as well as the transitions of freezing and melting. Moreover, we also see water vapor, mist, clouds, and steam. There are actually very few substances that we see in two, let alone three phases: solid, liquid and gaseous. Yes, we may have seen *demonstrations* of frozen nitrogen and we may know that mercury freezes at close to -40 degrees Celsius and Fahrenheit. But for most substances, it is rare that we are privileged to see it change phase. Most of us do not melt aluminum or vaporize mercury in our kitchen (neither of which I recommend!).

Water makes up most of the surface of the earth and most of the substance of our own bodies. Not only do we drink it and swim in it and dive into it and skate on it as ice; we use it to clean; we use it to mix with other things in industry as well as in our own kitchens.

The amount of water that falls in a region makes a huge difference in the flora and fauna that populate that area. As we all know, cacti dot the sands of hot deserts, while the rain forests favor a wider variety of trees, shrubs, moss, ferns and even plants that live on other plants. Naturally, animals that actually live in the water have adapted to living, loving, and dying in that water. We typically think of animal species as being subject to the laws of natural selection. Eventually, a species living in water must adapt to that watery environment (or go extinct). But, I believe evolution is a two-way street that also involves the *choices* that animals make. Let's see how.

Imagine a species of animal that lives on the edge of a pond in an otherwise arid region. Initially, they all belong to one species and, by definition, they can mate with each other. Let's call this species "tortles." In the same way that some people prefer the seashore while others like forests and still others like the desert, we would expect that *some* of these tortles really enjoy hanging out in the water. Others prefer the nearby desert and only come to the pond in order to drink. Over many eons, those who spend a lot of time in the water are likely to mate with other like-minded tortles. Those that love the desert will tend to find their mates from that sub-population. There will be a natural variation in bodies of these tortles with some having stronger shorter legs, for example, while others are born with longer legs and some might even have a slight webbing between their toes. When times are tough, the long-legged or web-toed tortles who like water will be able to swim better and have better luck finding food, escaping predators and hooking up with their mates. The web-toed variety on *land*, however, will not be so lucky. They will tend to get tiny pebbles stuck between their toes and have a harder time "racing" (if I may use that word for tortles) to beat out rivals to a mate or to escape predators. Meanwhile, the stocky legged tortles who live on land will have advantages on dry land. If, however, they choose to spend most of their time in the water, they will be at a disadvantage. After many generations, the tortles will actually drift into two completely different species. Eventually, the land tortles will no longer be able to mate with water-based tortles. Indeed, they may find the prospect very off-putting in their tortlely way. Similarly, the water tortles will no longer be able to mate with land tortles (and, yech, who would want to?). Eventually, though many similarities might remain, the water tortles would come to be what we now know as turtles and the land tortles would evolve into tortoises. What started as a tiny pebble of desire and preference, would over many millennia, ripple into wave after wave of evolutionary pressure, eventually resulting in two different species.

The reason I bring this up is that we often think of evolution as something that *happens to a species* in response to the environment and that is certainly a valid perspective. In some cases, the environment changes for various reasons and having a diverse population is a kind of "insurance" that *some* of the population will still be well-adapted to that new environment. If the change is too sudden or too drastic, the entire species will die. If the pond and the nearby desert were both to be suddenly covered in hot lava from a volcanic eruption, both the turtles and the tortoises would perish. However, if the

pond spread suddenly because of unusual flooding, only
the turtles would survive. On the other hand, if the pond
dried up for months at a time, only the tortoises would
likely survive.

Equally important however, is that over a long period of
time, the *conscious choices* or *preferences* of the tortles
play an important part in natural selection. The same
thing has been true for the entire 4.75 billion years of
evolutionary history of life on earth. What we humans
have become today is *partly* a *response* to environmental
pressures, but it is *also* partly because of the *choices and
preferences* of our ancestors.

There are two other important "levels" of choice and
adaptation. Within the life of an individual animal, much
is learned via a variety of mechanism. For example, if
your dog goes for a walk and you train him properly, he
will not yank your arm but walk with the lead
comfortably loose. A really well-trained dog might even
keep beside you under the extreme provocation of a
squirrel running by. If the dog continues to pull hard on
the leash despite your attempts to train him, you will
eventually find it too much work to take him for walks
and he will suffer physically from the lack of exercise.
Over longer periods of time, people as a whole will tend
to breed dogs so as to make them be more trainable rather
than less trainable. *Eventually, the ability of the
individual dogs to learn to adapt to their situations will
impact the evolution of the species.* A dog whose body is
adapted so that many walks are necessary for health will
be subject to a greater degree of evolutionary pressure
toward learning how to walk socially than will a dog

whose body allows a more sedentary life. Further, to the extent that dogs keep choosing to go for walks, those choices will impact both their learning and eventually their evolution (and ours).

There is yet another level of choice-evolution interaction. If a human *society* "choses" (via laws, customs, regulations, etc.) to reward one kind of behavior and punish another, the first kind of behavior will tend to be learned and the second not learned within the lifetime of an individual. Eventually, there will even be evolutionary pressure toward one kind of behavior (and body) and away from the other. For example, imagine a society that idealizes and rewards athletic excellence over artistic excellence. Athletes might make more money and have higher social status. They will tend to mate more often and eventually the whole species will tend to be more athletic. This might seem a tremendously good thing. In addition, if there is a huge population of athletes in a society, they may learn from each other and challenge each other toward ever greater feats of athletic prowess. Their bodies will tend to evolve biologically in various ways to support athletic activity. However, there is a down side too. In order to be a more successful athlete, the individual will have to take greater risks, spend a lot of time in athletic endeavors, and consume more food and water. If resources are scarce in a society, having everyone being athletic could be problematic. Other things being equal, there would tend to be less time spent in building shelters, caring for children, finding food, etc.

On the other hand, we can imagine a society that rewards artistic achievement over everything else. In this case, those who have a natural proclivity toward art will be rewarded in various ways; some will learn to be great artists. Typically, those who love art will spend more time doing it and therefore, over time, improve their skill. They will also develop *communities of practice* and learn from each other. We can imagine this society eventually developing rules and regulations as well as customs that favor artistic expression. In such a hypothetical monoculture society, a person of unusual athletic ability might not be much noticed while a person of unusual artistic ability would be. While it would certainly be nice to be surrounded by beautiful artwork all one's life, there are some potential down side risks to a society that concentrated all its efforts toward art. People might make shelters that looked beautiful but did not work very well. They might favor crops with beautiful flowers even if the resulting fruit was inedible, poisonous, or simply not very nutritious.

While the hypothetical examples above describe athletic and artistic endeavors, the same principles would apply toward any physical characteristic (being tall or short, being very strong or less so) or mental characteristic (being extremely curious, loving greatly, being cold-hearted). There are some situations and some aspects of various situations that favor any one mental or physical characteristic over another. And eventually the choices that the species makes about those characteristics that we most favor will come to be more prevalent in the population. Just as you were partly shaped by the choices made by every single one of your ancestors, so too do your choices today impact what kind of world your descendants will live in and therefore, eventually also determine what they are, how they look, and how they are prone to behave. And, because our modern society is so tightly interconnected in so many ways, your choices will not only impact what becomes of *your* descendants but also those of your neighbors and quite possibly what becomes of everyone on the planet. What an awesome responsibility! In the same way, the choices that your neighbors make will impact the world that your descendants will live in. That inter-relatedness of the impacts of choice can also be an awesome pain and a challenge for cooperation. You personally would not make some of the choices that your neighbors make and *vice versa*.

For example, I personally love nature. I have always loved going out into the woods or fields, and I feel better and more alive when I am outdoors. I would love it if we make the wild world livable forever. I would very much like to see people, a thousand generations from now, be able to experience trees, flowers, birds, and so on. I hate the idea that everything will end up as one giant city of plastic and metal. What kind of life would that be? Not one I would like and not one I would like for others. But not everyone agrees with my vision of the future. Some would see the endless world-filling mega-super-city-state as a great culmination of human progress.

In our current state of confusion about where civilization and our environment should be headed, the best we can do is to encourage the maximum amount of diversity. There certainly is no single world-wide shared vision of who we are and where we want to go and become. If there were, we could debate about the best way to get there, but we do not even have consensus on where we *should* be headed.

Here is just a small sample of the multitude of visions people seem to have about humanity's future. 1) We don't have to do anything. God has a plan and it will happen. 2) We need to grab all the resources for our country by whatever means necessary because the resources are limited and time is running out. 3) The government is out to get our guns but they won't succeed. 4) In a decade or two, AI will surpass human intelligence and tell us how to get out of the mess we're in. 5) In a few decades, AI will "take over" and destroy humanity. 6) All sovereign nations will work together toward peace and prosperity for all. 7) It's a dog eat dog world. Always was. Always will be. 8) We are evolving to a higher plane of non-physical and purely spiritual existence.

I didn't pick this particular set to make fun of anyone. My point is that these are just eight out of *thousands* that I could have listed. We clearly have extremely different ideas of where we want humanity to go! The fact that you have a vision shared by lots of other people and you're convinced it's the right one doesn't change the fact that not everyone has the same vision. Let's just take those specific ones. What do these various visions imply about what we should do in the real world of today? Who should we vote for? Where should we live? Should we recycle? How should we raise our children? What should we eat?

The thing is this. Let's face it. We humans have never been here before. For the longest time, we lived in little tribes of people. Each little tribe had over a thousand square miles to roam around in and do with what they pleased! The human population of the entire earth might have been a million for most of our time as a species. Now, earth has 7 *billion* people! If we had to hunt and gather for our food, the vast majority of us would die, full stop. We have technologies and speeds and greeds that were literally unimaginable to our ancestors. We've been following the scripts of different cultures for most of our individual lives and for most of our life as a species. Guess what. Now, the play, as scripted by our cultural heritage, is over, but here we are! We are still on stage!

We must *improvise. We don't know where we are headed or where we should be headed.* This is completely new ground! Don't be terrified because we don't know. Don't hold on tightly to a teeny corner. Grab the challenge. If we humans pull this off, it will be the greatest come-from-behind victory in the history of —well — anything.

Perhaps you recall, as I do, that in the most archaic memories, parents are *huge*! My mother was huge and my dad was huger! Of course, they not only loomed gigantic physically, they also had a huge influence on me. That, I never thought about as a child, but we'll return to influence later.

The other remarkable thing about my parents, in early memories, is how *different* they were from each other. My mother was soft, gentle, smooth-skinned with a soprano voice. My dad was completely different. He was larger, but besides that, he was hard, physical, hairy and his voice boomed so loud I could feel as well as hear the vibrations. They smelled completely different and I generally saw them at different times of the day, or, more accurately, I saw my mother most of the day and my dad only for small segments on most days. They *did* different things, *said* different things, held me differently. There was no way as a toddler that I saw them as two different examples of a larger class of things called "people." They were as different as night and oranges to me.

These differences were not just physical and perceptual. I also realized that the species of "Dad" and the species of "Mom" also behaved quite differently. For example, I could generally count on my dad to remain calm and to get things done whereas in an emergency, my mother generally fell to pieces emotionally. No, come to think of it, she *always* fell to pieces. Or, equally likely, she acted the dramatic part of someone falling to pieces.

For example, when I was about five years old, my parents took me to a stranger's house for one of their "Bridge Parties." To me, "Bridge" was a complete mystery. I understood the concept of games; e.g., "Mother May I", "Red Light Green Light", "Pick Up Sticks", "Checkers", and (my personal favorite), "Red Rover, Red Rover." In "Red Rover, Red Rover," the opposing team formed a human chain by holding hands. Everyone on a team would chant in unison, "Red Rover, Red Rover, let Tommy come over." (Tommy was my nick-name at the time). There were two really cool parts to this game in addition to the chanting. One, when it was your turn to make a human chain, you might get to hold hands with a pretty girl. Two, when you were called, you were allowed, indeed *encouraged*, to run as fast you could, and then SMASH right into the opposing team! That was fun! Honestly, I think I'd like to do that right now. But Bridge? The adults just took turns throwing cards on the table. Yet, they were generally screaming and laughing while playing this game. They seemed to be enjoying themselves but I had no idea why. So far as I could tell, no-one playing bridge ever got to hold hands with a pretty girl let alone run across the room and smash into people. Adult fun, to me, seemed anything but.

In any case, however much Mom and Dad enjoyed "Bridge Club", I certainly didn't. My parents took me into some random bedroom and said, "you will sleep in here." Right. I'm five years old in a strange place and I am supposed to go to sleep while a mini-version of Woodstock roars on about ten feet from my five year old (and therefore highly sensitive) ears. No, I'm not going to sleep. Even as a five year old, I knew that wasn't in the cards. I'm not sure how my parents could have deluded themselves that I would, but apparently they managed. Since sleep was out of the question, I needed to find some way to occupy myself. What I can *do*? I asked myself and I answered myself: I'm going to explore the room!

I rather liked the room. It had wall to wall carpeting and dark, heavy, solid wood furniture. I padded about the room looking at this and that, but there wasn't much to see, really. That is what necessitated me to go to phase two of exploring the room; that is, looking *under* things and *in* things. I looked under the bed, but it was just dusty. I knew it was a long shot that anyone else was trying to invent a new color and keeping the best results under the bed in empty little maraschino cherry jars, but you never know. Well, actually, yes, eventually I *did* know. But I didn't know *then* because I didn't know that many people so I didn't really know how many might be trying to invent new colors. Since then, I've met many people who do exactly that although not quite so literally as I was trying to do way back then. I have many grandchildren and every one of them is inventing new colors, each in their unique way.

Disappointment haunted my initial explorations of the bedroom bureau. Drawer after drawer was filled with clothes. Sigh. Then — my eyes actually did become as big as saucers. Large saucers. Because lying right there atop some boring gray gaberdine pants was the *coolest* and *biggest* gun I had ever seen! I liked my guns! In fact, one of my earliest memories was of a red plastic one. But now, as a "big boy," I had metal guns. Even better, when

I pulled the trigger, they went "BAM!" "BAM!" because of the caps. I liked my own guns all right, but *this* gun was *way, way cooler.* For one thing, it was *all* metal. Mine were partly plastic. And, the gun was shiny with a depth of its own — except for the handle which had a wonderful pebbled grain.

I would have loved just *looking* at that black gun for an hour. But, of course, I had to pick it up. Well, if the look of that gun had been exquisite, and it was, the *feel* of the gun thrilled me, filled me with uncertain terrors never felt before — to quote Mr. Poe. But alongside the terror was admiration that quickly blossomed into an actual physical love. The object that constituted the gun seemed so beautifully and solidly built. Had I ever before held something that heavy and dense? I didn't think so.

I knew that my parents had told me to stay in the room and go to sleep. But they were the two people I loved most in the universe. How could I allow the discovery of something this cool, go unshared? I had to let them find out just how cool this gun was. I probably also thought that no little credit would be coming my way for being the discoverer of this marvelous instrument. (Somehow, it never once crossed my mind that the people who owned the house probably already knew about this gun). I definitely thought of it as *my* discovery, and so it was, in a way. And, if I was never going to get any credit from my Grandpa for inventing a new color, at least I would have this great exploratory accomplishment forever written into the plus column of my life's ledger.

Out into the living room that bubbled with laughing, screaming adults somehow enjoying "Bridge" I tottered, slightly off balance from the weight of the gun, though I was able to hold it one hand, just the way the cowboys and policemen did. "Look what *I* found." Now, listening to the memory of how I said it, I realize it probably was getting credit for my discovery rather than sharing it that most motivated me. Ah, well. Live and learn, as they say. I expected to gain some credit for my discovery and some appreciation for the gun, but I never expected the eruption of adult action and concern and panic and fear and anger and utter surprise. I walked into a room of laughter. That laughter popped like an over-sized soap bubble. Instead, a palpable wave of negativity washed over me. I felt such a sensory overload that my memory is like a loud noise and a great white light. Not only did I receive zero plaudits for my wonderful discovery, I definitely had done something *unspeakably* wrong. (Later, I was told that the gun had been loaded with the safety off). But at the time, I felt only bewildered disappointment. However, the one thing I do recall through the white noise was that Dad remained calm and managed to take the gun from me without my testing it out on him for fun. Meanwhile, Mom was being her usual "hysterical in an emergency" self.

At the time, I did not think that my mother was "typical" of all women nor did I think that she was "atypical." It's just that I knew this about my mother, but my mother formed one edge or point on the growing conceptual map of people. And, everything that was true about her was all there together in her own rather large corner of my mind: soft, smooth, soprano, hysterical, gentle, slightly hard of hearing, illogical, loving, beautiful, and fun. Her body positively writhed when she found something funny. Early on, I tried to learn how to cause one of those paroxysms of laughter. Dad, on the other hand, could be counted on in a crisis. He was also hard and hairy and loud and undemonstrative. When, he laughed, most of the time, it was "UH!" That's it! One burst of sound: half snort, half laugh. I do that too sometimes. On the other hand, I also go into a full out writhe with laughter as well. I am part Mom; part Dad just as most of us are with respect to our parents.

My parents had two different professions as well. Dad was an engineer. He was very logical; yes, even as a very young kid I saw this. Mom was an English and Drama teacher. Years later, at CHI in Atlanta, talking with Doug Engelbart, I discovered that his parents had had the same combination of professions. As an adult, I can imagine that their professions not only seemed to be choices that sprung from their native talents, but that the professions, in turn, helped cement these traits.

I met other family members at a young age and every one of them was quite different. My mother's mother, Ada was smart, soft, and she told me "Old Pete" stories. We listened to radio programs together such as *The Lone Ranger, Roy Rogers, Hop-along Cassidy*, and *Tom Corbett and the Space Cadets*. Grandma was the Superintendent of Sunday School at the Methodist church we attended. She also founded the Firestone Park Dramatic Club and ran it for decades. Meetings were held at my grandparents' house and the women (all the members were women) read plays. This turned out to be a cool deal for me because, as a little kid, whenever someone didn't show up, I filled in. My memory was so good, that even without trying, I knew all the parts. Grandma also had to take "iron shots" because she was anemic. The best thing though was that she baked peanut butter cookies and when she made a pie, she made butter, sugar, and cinnamon roll-ups!

Her obituary from the Akron Beacon Journal begins this way: "Ada Weimer: Founder Of Drama Club Mrs. Ada P. Weimer, 78, founder of the Firestone Park Dramatic Club and its director for 30 years, died at Edwin Shaw Hospital Wednesday after a six-month illness. Born in Akron, Mrs. Weimer, 1384 Grant St., attended Greensburg High School and Heidelberg College. For many years, she was a Sunday school superintendent at Firestone Park Methodist Church, of which she was a member." Apart from that, it lists her three sons and daughter whom she "left behind."

No mention of her peanut butter cookies though. Occasionally, after much begging, she would also make popcorn "from scratch" in a kettle. Not mentioned in her obituary. She also spent a lot of time canning for the extensive "root cellar" my grandparents had in their basement. Not mentioned. Sometimes, she would walk with me up Grant Street to meet Grandpa at the bus stop. On the way, she never failed to scowl at the "beer joint" up the street where the overwhelming odor of beer and alcohol would flood out onto the street. Not mentioned. On rainy days, Grandma would take out two large shoe boxes that contained her extensive post card collection. Each had a photo, or more rarely, a cartoon, on one side and a hand-written or hand-printed note on the other side. They had come from many US states and from many countries around the world. The foreign ones also had interesting stamps to ponder with miniature scenes or portraits or animals from far-away places. I found all of it fascinating: the varieties of handwriting, the stamps, the pictures, the addresses. I would often ask her who these people were and what their comments meant. Usually, she would answer, but occasionally she wouldn't. The newspaper obituary kept silent on the whole matter. Not one single post card was cited.

Grandma was affectionate as was her sister Mary, but their sister Emma "took the cake." She was forever pawing, fawning, making a fuss, telling me nursery rhymes, hugging, kissing, etc. All three of these women were somewhat overweight and typically wore loose print dresses. I tend to think of my grandmother mainly wearing white, or off-white dresses with small flowers printed on them. Mary, on the other hand, the largest of the three, tended to wear dark blue dresses with white flowers. Emma typically wore brown or yellow dresses but made up for it with bright red lipstick and lots of make up. That entire branch of the family held family reunions every year. Much later, I met a cousin of Mom's that had grown up with her family for a time. He eventually became a psychology professor at an Ivy League School. Although I met numerous distant uncles and cousins over the years, I don't much recall much about these more distant relatives. Grandma's mother had come from Wales. My Grandpa painted a picture of the Welsh cottage that she was born in. It was beautiful and set in beautiful country but quite modest in size.

Now, speaking of Grandpa, he was as different and distinct from Grandma as Mom was from Dad. Grandpa smelled of pipe tobacco and although he too, like Dad, seldom laughed very demonstrably, he always seemed to have a twinkle in his grey eyes. Grandpa was extremely smart and knew about everything; or so it seemed at the time. Besides that, he was multi-talented. He worked as an engineer, but he was also an artist of some note. He was also an accomplished musician. Best of all, from my perspective, he was an excellent teacher. When we went out to the garden to pick corn on the cob, he taught me something about plants, soil or gardening. Einstein died when I was almost ten years old. Grandpa showed me the item about it in the Akron Beacon Journal and then proceeded to tell me about Einstein's work (in elementary terms). He subscribed to *Sky and Telescope* as well as *The Atlantic Monthly* and *Scientific American* and the magazine of the American Museum of Natural History. He would point out particular articles to me and then discuss them with me or explain something in more detail.

There's no need to describe every single person in my family. The main point is that *each* of these people seemed very *very* different from the others. As an adult, I can now see many "family resemblances" in terms of their skills, interests, psychology and physical characteristics. But as a child, I perceived none of that. It never even occurred to me that we all needed to breathe or had two arms and two legs. If someone had asked me, I could have answered correctly, of course, but the similarities among these people never spontaneously crossed my mind. Every week, I listened as The Lone Ranger and Tonto found someone in trouble, tracked down the bad guys, shot a gun out of their hand and rode away. After they were gone, the beneficiaries of their bravery would remark that they didn't know the true identity of The Lone Ranger, but that he had left behind a single silver bullet. In retrospect, these stories were quite formulaic. But at the time, every story was just a different story. And so it was with folks in my family. They were different. They were individuals. Beyond that, they collectively made up the space of possible individuals as I then perceived it.

As childhood continued, of course, that people-space continued to grow. New people often revealed, not just that people could be more extreme on dimensions I knew such as age, size, or how much they laughed, but they forced me to consider and construct entirely new dimensions as well. People, it turned out, came in different colors; they spoke with different accents. In fact, they spoke in entirely different languages!

When I was about three and a half, Mom, Dad and I all left for Portugal. My Mom told me later that I was frustrated that a bunch of Greek sailors on the ship could not communicate with me. I don't recall this. But I do recall a little of learning to speak Portuguese although to me, it was not "learning to speak a different language." It was just that I encountered people who spoke differently and I learned to communicate with them. Some people don't laugh much while others laugh quite a lot. Similarly, some people spoke the way I was used to and others spoke some entirely different way. It never occurred to me, as a child, that they spoke an entirely different language and certainly not that they spoke that strange other way because of their own family and their own country. If asked, I imagine that I might have answered that they *chose* to speak Portuguese rather than English. But mainly, it just *was*. I didn't consider *why* people were fat or skinny; why they spoke with an accent or not; why some people were male and some female; why some were old and some were young. Each person was simply and completely the way they were. They went about their business and as I interacted with them they punched at the edges of the net of my ideas about what people were like. Each person punched outwards in their own direction and the space of people grew larger and larger and larger.

I guess not everyone reacts that same way. It now seems to me, as an adult, that some people only expand their space of people a little ways from the points laid down by their first family and friends. When someone is too different, they are not really part of the whole human condition, but instead, are assigned to some other category such as "old person" or "toddler" or "professional athlete" or "foreigner" or "cripple" or "gay." For some, each category requires special treatment different from all the rest. If, for instance, a "professional athlete" assaults or rapes someone, that might be okay because there are special rules for such folks. If, on the other hand, a "foreigner" assaults or rapes someone, they should at least be put in prison and quite possibly killed in some particularly horrendous way.

Indeed, even my own family gave some hints that this was the right way to think about people. You had to be careful with grandparents because they were "old" and could be easily injured or broken into small pieces. When my cousin threw a xylophone across the room and hit me in the head, no punishment was forthcoming because he was "just a little kid" and "didn't know any better." When I went to the hospital, people did not seem to be treated as people at all but rather given epithets based on their disease; e.g., "the pneumonia" or "the burn victim" or "the appendicitis." Given names were rarely used. Although, even as an adult, I see that while there are commonalities in the way doctors need to treat patients with particular diseases, it seems to me that there are also often important differences as well. It seems very distancing to call a person by their disease.

One important way that people differ from each other is how they treat and categorize other people. To me, every new individual I meet still seems quite different from any of the others. Everyone is unique. Everyone has a name. None of us really wants to be lumped into a category and then treated according to that category rather than who they really are. Yet, it is easy to fall into the trap of doing exactly that with others. Our planet is too small and too interconnected to continue with that. We didn't necessarily choose up sides, but we're on the same team, like it or not. If we don't get along in this giant human family, then there won't be any human family left.

16 FAMILY MATTERS 2: GARLIC CLOVES & PUFFER FISH

Certainly, there are many "how to" books out there that would lead you to believe that the only thing that stands between you and owning the universe is your attitude. It isn't a totally bad thing to imagine that you can do anything and have no limitations due to circumstances or your innate abilities and predispositions. It's a fiction, of course. It's a complete and utter fiction. If you spent the first five years of your life drinking lead tainted water, e.g., no amount of the proper "attitude" is going to undo the harm. But, for people whose main obstacle to a fulfilled life is self-doubt, it could provide a good mantra.

What I have in mind however, is something different; *viz.*, trying to show how family situations tend to be continuous threads in a way that is analogous to the continuous genetic threads. For example, my grandmother used to tell "Old Pete" stories and ran a dramatic club. My mother became an English and Drama teacher. I have always loved acting and storytelling. Several of my kids and grandkids have also written originally and extensively. My mother's brothers were all jokesters and storytellers. Her oldest brother Karl was a principal and then superintendent of schools. The middle boy, Bob, became a psychiatrist. The youngest, Paul, became a lawyer. The next generation included two psychologists, two lawyers, a neurosurgeon, a teacher. I could elaborate further but the point is that storytelling, art, psychology, and education as well as science and engineering are threads throughout this very local part of my family tree.

I need to explain why I subtitled this, "Garlic Cloves and Puffer Fish." As preface, it's good to remember that both garlic and puffer fish are *our* distant cousins. The same basic machinery that makes the cells of a garlic plant "work" and live and reproduce is what does all those same things in our cells. And our other, somewhat less distant cousin, the Puffer Fish, has that same machinery in every one of its cells. Beyond that cellular similarity, we even share most of the same organs and types of symmetry as the Puffer (or any other) Fish. I bring up our relation to these distant cousins because I would like to have you view what I am about to say about various people as being observational and not rendering value judgments. It would be silly to go out to a garlic plant and yell, "Why can't you be more like a Puffer Fish?! What's wrong with you?!" It would be equally ridiculous, of course, to go snorkeling and when you encounter a Puffer Fish scream at it: "What are you doing out here in the ocean? Why can't you be more like your cousin Garlic who at least makes wonderful tasting (to most) and health-giving nutrients? No, instead, you poison people! What's wrong with you?"

Now, when it comes to people, of course, it isn't just their genes that determines behavior. The family, neighborhood, culture, religion, and physical environment that they grow up in determines, at least in large measure, who they become. Humans come in many varieties. This is both because, when it comes to our own life, we can actually make ourselves different in some ways on purpose (there is a grain of truth in the "positive thinking will win you everything you want" genre) and secondly, when it comes to someone perceiving us, their own background and character will determine what they see in you or me. Similarly, your background will help determine what you see in others. If you think back on your own experience, you'll see this is true. Among the many ways that people differ is how neatness-oriented they are. The hit TV series, The Odd Couple, featured two bachelors living together; one was an utter slob (Oscar) and the other was a neat-nick (Felix). We all probably know people close to those extremes. You may even know two such people in your own family. I'm not trying to say one of these characteristics is better or worse than the other. But I would like to point out that each makes a lot of sense, under certain conditions.

Some years ago, I was watching a TV program about Alice Waters, a famous chef, restaurant owner, and author. She believes in such things as organic, locally grown ingredients. In any case, she happened to make this offhand comment that "it didn't really matter if a little piece of the garlic skin clings to a clove" {at least in the context of the sauce they were making for a huge fish}. Anyway, I do most of the cooking in my house and I do try to remove the skin of garlic cloves. Most of the time, it's fairly easy. But every once in a while I have encountered a clove of garlic that is as pathologically stubborn about giving up its skin as a corrupt politician is about giving up the illusion of sanctity. Even a garlic plant has its own personality, I suppose. On the scale of neat-nick to slob, I would put myself near the middle. Of course, to anyone who thinks it's good to be super neat, I will seem like a slob. And to anyone who thinks cleaning is just not worth the trouble, I may seem like a neat-nick.

Anyway, my point is that maybe there comes a point where you don't generally have to be absolutely precise in cooking. And I would guess that this rings true with your experience as well. There are some cooks whose approach is very intuitive and, although they may follow a recipe, their measurements may not be totally accurate. And, then there are cooks who will follow directions extremely carefully. Generally speaking, it doesn't make that much difference. I tend to prefer dishes such as mixed ginger/curry vegetables, burritos, or omelets. In these dishes, I can get away with a huge variation in proportions and specific ingredients. I give these dishes care and attention to detail, but all within very broad parameters.

In at least one case, however, it is crucial to be a "neat-nick" cook and that is in the preparation of the Puffer Fish. The Puffer Fish contains a highly potent neurotoxin called tetrodotoxin. Most of this toxin resides in the liver, skin, and other internal organs. It is very easy if you are even the least bit sloppy — and we are not talking Oscarian sloppihood, just normal college guy sloppihood — to nick something and release the poison into the flesh making it potentially deadly. Under those circumstances, being a neat-nick is literally vital. In some cases, expert chefs push a little further and allow a tiny bit of the toxin to bleed into the flesh which will cause a "high" in the eater, but not be fatal. Personally, I think I'll stick with tuna. The point is that being extremely neat and careful can be a very good thing. Packing your parachute — good to be careful! Performing cataract surgery — be precise!

On the other hand, suppose that you are spear fishing or out gathering nuts. A "neat-nick" might want to make sure every fish is skewered in exactly the same way. Except, perhaps for Puffer Fish, it doesn't matter that much; the point is to catch the fish. Similarly, if you are gathering walnuts, there generally isn't much point in arranging them by slight variations in size.

Suppose you are making a rock wall. You would do well to make sure it doesn't fall down but the way to do that is by careful arrangement and filling in the cracks carefully with cement. An alternative approach is to insist that every rock is exactly the same. This would make building the wall much easier. On the other hand, it would be absurdly time consuming to search for rocks of precisely the same size. Other approaches are to have one group of people cut rocks to preset measures and then the job of building the walls is easier or to make artificial rocks called "bricks." Under various circumstances, any of these methods will work just fine. In other circumstances, any of these approaches might fail. It isn't quite so simple a matter as Disney and the Three Little Pigs would have you believe.

When it comes to recipes, whether for bricks or for soufflés, it is difficult to know ahead of time which aspects of the process require a Felixian attention to detail and which aspects are fine for a more Oscarian approach. And, just as there are situations that are particularly suitable and best done by neat-nicks there are other situations particularly well suited to slobs. This same principle holds true for every approach and personality trait that I can think of. So when I describe people in my extended family, I am not trying to pass judgement on who is better than whom. You might imagine that there is an attempt on my part to make out someone as "bad" or "good" based on your own personality preferences. Similarly, it's quite possible that I accidentally make one or the other kind of personality sound better than they really are based on my own preferences.

Although it is quite natural for people to express different preferences on the neat-nick to slob dimension, it is often a source of tension, argument, fights, and in extreme cases, probably divorce and murder. Most often, when an "Oscar" does something annoyingly sloppy, Felix will not try to dialogue about the situation and negotiate a solution. Rather, Felix's first move is more often to call out Oscar's *character* as being deficient because he is such a slob. Immediately and quite predictably, Oscar's defenses go up. His next move is to point out that Felix is insanely OCD (Obsessive-Compulsive Disorder). And thus, their disagreement moves from what is immediate, simple, and fixable to one that is long-term, complex, and unfixable. Oscar will never convince Felix to be like Oscar and Felix will not ever convince Oscar to be like Felix. In fact, for Felix to even expect Oscar to act Felixian (or *vice versa)* is rather silly.

You have undoubtedly heard the expression that you "marry the family" as well as your spouse. I found this unfathomably silly when I was younger, but now I see that in many ways it is true. For example, if your spouse has unresolved issues from their childhood, those can impact your relationship. If your spouse's family is into crime or drugs or unnecessary drama, those will certainly impact you. These people will almost certainly interact with you and your kids so they will impact your lives both directly and indirectly.

Keeping all this in mind, let's tune in to "Uncle Al." Al worked at one point as a commercial artist. In such a position, being something of a "Felix" probably worked to his benefit. But not every situation calls for OCD. Al lived in one of two houses at the end of a dead end street. What would you do if you drove to the end of his narrow, dead end street? Well, one possible action would be to abandon your car at the end of the street and walk home to buy another car or just wait there until you were beamed up by aliens. Most people however, would instead go into one of the two driveways at the end of the street, turn their car around and drive back out the dead end street. Al didn't like that. I suppose most of us might be mildly annoyed. But after all, what else could people realistically do? So, while most people might be a little annoyed at strangers using their driveway for a U-turn maneuver, Al was instead, *incensed*. So annoyed was Uncle Al that he paid to have five steel posts put into the end of his drive. Indeed, this completely prevented any stranger from using his driveway as a place to turn around. Chalk one up for Uncle Al.

Now, you may have detected a slight flaw in Al's plan. *He* could no longer use his driveway either. For that matter, he could no longer use his garage to house his car. But to Al's way of thinking, that was worth it because he had achieved his goal. The phrase, "cutting off one's nose to spite one's face" comes to mind. At another point, several of my ex-brothers-in-laws went over to clean Uncle Al's house. When they opened up the refrigerator, the shelves were all filled with the same thing. Can you guess what it was? No, you probably can't. Every shelf was filled with tiny paper mini-ramekins. And in each of those tiny paper mini-ramekins was tartar sauce. Upon questioning, the story finally came out. Every Friday, Al went to a nearby diner where they had an "all you can eat fish" special. The fish came with tartar sauce. Uncle Al *hated* tartar sauce. But he had *paid* for the tartar sauce! So, when he left the restaurant, he took the tartar sauce with him each and every time.

This seems a little on the crazy side, but I would guess that almost everyone has sometimes taken something that they have access to even though they ended up not using it. In fact, it's a little odder and more selfish than that. We might even know when we take the items that it's very unlikely we use them. For example, in the IBM cafeteria, I would often take an extra napkin. Why? Because on rare occasions, someone, possibly even me, would spill something and having an extra napkin that could be deployed jack-knife quick proved very handy. But most of the time, these hypothetical emergencies failed to eventuate. Now, what to do with the extra napkin? I could put it in the trash, or since it was clean, put it in the recycling. To me, taking the time and effort to recycle is completely worth it. Not everyone does that. We can return to that later, but re-use (or in this case, first use) trumps recycling. So, I would take the napkins back to my office. I had one drawer in particular that ended up with a collection of napkins as well as tea bags, plastic forks, tiny packets of salt and pepper, and other food-related items. Small stuff. There were no stashes of candy bars or soda cans or deer carcasses.

However, this example of hoarding was not an idle and useless exercise. When people in the lab had birthdays or other types of celebration, it actually turned out to be quite handy to have a nearby supply of napkins and plastic forks. When I thought about the design rationale for this procedure, I never thought to myself, "I paid for this dinner and there's no rule against taking two napkins, so I want to keep what is mine." In terms of explanation, my saving napkins and Uncle Al's taking tartar sauce are light-years apart. But looked at in terms of situations and behavior, there are actually many similarities.

As already explained, all of us are closely related. Although Uncle Al was not "related" in the way that people generally use that word, our ancestors were common for billions of years. So, I would hypothesize that the behavior of keeping something that is not of immediate use but might be used in the future is one that is found broadly in the animal kingdom and in plants. We imagine that the desert plant that stores water in it's thick leaves does not "think about it." It seems pretty silly to think it thinks at all. But let's expand the idea of how information is coded just a little. It wouldn't make a difference if the rationale were written in Spanish or English or French would it? It wouldn't matter if the design rationale were printed in 14 point Helvetica or 12 point Times New Roman. It wouldn't matter whether it was coded in ascii or EBCDIC. So, why not extend the concept a little further. The "design rationale" for the plant's behavior is coded in it's DNA. We may not be able to "read" this design rationale quite as readily as we could read one printed in our native language. But that is basically a matter of convenience, not a matter of underlying truth. The plant *does* have a design rationale for being "greedy."

When it comes to human behavior, of course, there are not only genetic determiners but also social ones. (Actually, this can be true of non-human animals as well). So, it isn't just that people may have a genetic propensity for keeping extra items for future use; their particular culture has inculcated values and design rationals and ethics around greed, waste, generosity, and so forth. The design rationale that Al gave, I find too self-centered for my taste. My Mom was generous to a fault. And, when I say she was generous to a "fault" what I mean is that she was so generous that she would often give away the same item to several people. So, perhaps being overly generous can be a fault?

In any case, just as people come in all sizes and shapes, they come in all kinds of behavioral predispositions. These predispositions probably depend on genetics, culture, and family upbringing. There is no one "right answer" as to which characteristics are "best" under all circumstances. Some may innately be predisposed to Felixism while others may become that way because of strict teachings by their parents and schools. Regardless of why Felix is a neat-nick, Oscar is never going to convince him that he (Felix) should be like Oscar. That was true in paragraph 11 and it is still true in paragraph 17. One thing should be clear to both Felix and Oscar: *if* they can learn to work together effectively, they will be able to solve a wider range of problems than they would working alone. Often, of course, "working together" will mean that they are working toward a common goal, but in very different capacities. We might imagine Oscar & Felix to work for a large company; Oscar gets to be a happy-go-lucky sales person while Felix is better off doing the financials or testing the product.

Creativity, diversity and respect for differences have always been vital for people to cooperate, but it has probably never more important than it is in the 21st Century. Humanity has changed so much in thousands of external ways in the last two thousand years. Most of that change has been since the industrial revolution and most of *that* after the computer revolution. Change is not only rapid, it is becoming more rapid. Change in media, language, meaning are all happening more and more rapidly. In times of great change and great uncertainty, it has always seemed to me to absolutely and vitally important to include every viewpoint on the problem that we possibly can.

If I am lying on the beach under a sunny sky, feeling healthy and happy, I don't really need your advice much; at least, not this second. Yes, I may not be as neat as you would like or I am far too neat but I don't really care and it doesn't matter. You be you, and I'll be me. So long as I don't litter on *your* beach towel and you don't insist on my towel being as neat as yours, we can "live and let live."

On the other hand, if I am thrown into something beyond my comprehension, I would want to have as many eyes, ears, and mental predispositions on the problem as possible. Of course, it feels more comfortable to surround yourself only with those who already agree with you rather than a highly diverse group. You won't argue as much about what the problem is or about what "fairness" really means or even argue about what the right process is for combining your insights. A diverse group can initially provide a layer of added awkwardness for some.

In my experience, when people are focused on a situation or a problem, they get past that awkwardness very quickly and problem solving is enhanced. There are more ideas generated; the ideas are higher quality ideas; the evaluation of ideas is more robust; the group generates more ways to fit ideas together. Not only is the output of the group improved. It is just plain more fun during the entire process. Perhaps a better term would be to say that it is more engaging. If someone has a slight accent, you need to listen more closely. If someone comes from a different background, not only do they provide a different way of looking at things or even solution; they also stretch your mind. It may not be as broadening as traveling to another culture, but it is more than one step in that direction. An all-celery salad gets old fast, no matter how crisp the celery is.

Beyond all that, it seems important to remember that these variations in human predisposition are not entirely new human inventions. Many species of plants and animals exhibit different "philosophies" or "strategies" for dealing with the same issues: getting food and water, finding a mate, reproducing, avoiding predators, etc. (Yes, even plants do these things). What works for a plant in one climate will not do in another climate. Of course, it isn't just the climate. It also depends on what other species are present, the nature of the soil, etc. Some plants, for instance, put time and energy into making flowers to attract bees, having the bees fertilize the flowers, grow the fertilized flower into a fruit that is both colorful and tasty. This means the fruit (e.g., wild strawberries or raspberries) are eaten by our cousins the rabbits and then carried forth in many directions out and away from tree. The rabbits excrete the digested seeds which now find themselves in a tiny pre-fertilized plot. Come on! How about a hand of applause? Do you see how many ducks have be lined up her for this plan to work?

Can you imagine designing such a scheme in a business context? I had something of a reputation for "crazy ideas" but this? This is my craziest idea on psychotropic drugs and then put through a cognitive blender. I worked in "Corporate America" for about 40 years. I worked for IT companies. No-one would pay for research into an idea as convoluted as this one. So many things have to "line up" just right! How does the plant "know" what will attract the rabbit? How does it "know" how to make a flower that will attract bees? Of course, the flower needs to be constructed, not only to *attract* the bees but also constructed so that the bee visit will pollinate the flower! Evolution is slow but ultimately, a very clever process. That tree of living things? That's *our* tree. And that little teeny branch way over there? That includes Oscar and Felix and everyone else regardless of gender, age, race, religion, or how much they like to hoard, organize, or spread things around. Does it really make sense for us to destroy our whole branch of the tree of life just because we don't all want to go in exactly the same direction? And what about how our decisions affect every other part of the tree? Is it right for us to destroy other species for convenience or sport? If we don't do something different pretty quickly, we will destroy what we do not yet understand and reap the consequences after it's too late to undo them. We need to have a "family meeting" about whether it's okay to destroy our ecosystem.

It is, after all, a family matter.

17 FAMILY MATTERS 3: THE WHOLE IS GREATER THAN THE SUM OF THE PARTS

Some my earliest and fondest memories centered around family dinners at my grandpa and grandma's house. For Thanksgiving, for example, there was turkey, mashed potatoes, gravy, sweet potatoes, green beans, olives, rolls, salad and several pies for dessert. Beyond the vast array of food, it was fun to see my grandparents, parents, three aunts and three uncles, and various cousins. On a few occasions, my second cousin George appeared and early on my Aunt Mary and Aunt Emma. All of these people were so different! We had more fun because we were all there together.

You have heard "The Whole is Greater than the Sum of its Parts" before, no doubt, but I think this applies to a family setting as well. All families argue (although ours never did in these larger holiday settings.) And, almost all families love. But a fundamental question is this: do the people in the family tend to "thrive" more than they would on their own? If the family is functional, this should be the case. They balance each other; they support each other; they help each other improve. They cooperate when it counts. You will not always agree on everything. Far from it. You might be a slob like Oscar while your sibling might be very Felix-like. And, you're both "right" under different circumstances and for different tastes.

Many sports teams will have a variety of people who excel more in running, or in blocking, or in throwing, or scoring. In baseball, for instance, or American Football, there are very different people in different roles, both physically and temperamentally. An offensive lineman in football will typically be stronger and bigger than a quarterback. Moreover, if the lineman gets "angry", they might be able to block better on the next play. By contrast, the quarterback must remain calm, cool, and confident under pressure. He must try to put away any fear or anger or depression he feels on the way to the huddle before he gets there and certainly before the snap. When teams are working well together, they don't criticize each other for differences and they work together to win the game rather than wasting time pointing fingers or trying to assign blame. In a baseball or football team, there is no question that the individual does better because of his teammates. Working together they can solve problems, win trophies, and have more fun than they could individually.

In a similar vein, but at a different level, your right eye sees the world a little differently from your left eye. Thank goodness! Your brain normally integrates these two somewhat different, flat, 2-D pictures into a 3-D picture! Your brain does not argue as to which one of these views is "correct." It certainly does not instigate religious wars over it.

I say that the brain "normally" performs this magic. However, if a person is born and their eyes do not move or align smoothly, or if one eye is extremely near-sighted, it can happen that the brain "chooses" only one eye to pay attention to. In this case, it seems the two images are so discrepant that the brain "gives up" trying to integrate them. In a condition such as "amblyopia" the brain mainly relies on the input from one eye. This condition is a distinct disadvantage in many sports.

In boxing, for example, it is literally a show-stopper. A fighter might look like hamburger, but the fight goes on. If, however, there is a cut above his or her eye so that blood drips down to obscure vision in one eye, the fight is stopped. That fighter can no longer see in depth (as well as losing some peripheral vision). It is no longer deemed a "fair" fight. Anyway, it seems the human brain does have some limits as to how much two discrepant views can be reconciled, at least when it comes to vision. Is there a limit to how much a family may disagree productively and still be functional? This is a good question; one to return to later. Let's first turn to what are called "dysfunctional families."

We said in a functional family or team, people are better off than they would be doing something on their own. On the other hand, consider a dysfunctional family. Here, people get mostly grief, judgement, criticism, competition, and lies. Why does this happen? Often dysfunctional behaviors are handed down from generation to generation through social learning. If too many dysfunctional behaviors are in one family, this causes a "vicious circle" that makes things worse and worse. For example, imagine a family is basically healthy but they do not engage in "alternatives thinking." They see a situation, come up with an idea, and unless there is imminent danger, execute the idea as soon as possible.

They will often end up in a lot of trouble with that strategy; e.g., balancing on a pile of furniture to change a light bulb. However, if they don't engage in blame-finding, but instead they engage in collective improvement, they will learn over time to make fewer and fewer mistakes. People will all benefit from being in the family. But if a family instead fails to consider multiple alternatives before committing to a course of action *and* has a cycle of blaming each other without ever improving, then it will be dysfunctional. People will give more and get less in return than if they have been working alone. That does not mean there are zero benefits within a dysfunctional family. They may still cover for each other, help each other, provide emotional support, etc. But the costs outweigh the benefits in the long run.

People who come from functional families tend to see the world in a very different way from people who come from dysfunctional families. Obviously, there are all sorts of exceptions as well as other factors at play, but other things being equal, our families of origin color our perceptions of daily life and predispose us to certain actions. Depending on the circumstances, it is even true that some of what we think of as "dysfunction" could actually be "function" instead. Suppose, for instance, you and two siblings suddenly found yourself attacked by a bear. It may be the best thing imaginable to take the first action you think of without trying to over-analyze the situation. Or not. It may well depend on the bear. And, therein lies the rub.

Our own personal experiences are always a teeny sliver of all possible situations. So, your experience with a bear, bee, or bank may be quite different from mine. As a consequence, we may have different ideas about what constitutes function or dysfunction. In terms of the argument I am about to make, it doesn't really matter which is "better" or "worse." All that matters is that we agree some families provide a healthier environment than others. Attitudes are not all that are handed down; so are "ways to do things."

Perhaps the arbitrary nature of what we consider "intelligent" wisdom handed down in families is best illustrated by a story about making a Holiday Ham. In the kitchen, a 10 year old boy asks: "How come you're slicing off the ends of the ham?"

His mom answers, "Oh, that's the way your grandpa always did it."

Son: "So, why did he do it?"

Mom: "Oh, well. Uh. I don't really know. Let's go ask him."

Son: "Hey, Grandpa, how come you cut the ends of the ham off?"

Grandpa: "Well, sonny. It's because….it's because…let's see. That's the way my mom always did it."

As it turns out, the 90 year old great-grandma was at the feast as well. Though she was a bit hard of hearing, they eventually got her to understand the question and thus she answered, "Oh, I always used to cut off the ends because I only had one small pan and otherwise, it wouldn't fit. No reason for you all to do it now."

And there you have it in a nutshell. We are all walking around with thousands if not millions of little bits of "folk wisdom" we learned through our family interactions. In most cases, we're not even aware of them. We seldom ask about where this folk wisdom came from. Have any of us actually *tested* one of these behavioral "family heirlooms" in our own life to see whether it still works? And then what? Are you going to inform the others in the family that what everyone believes *may not actually be true*, at least in every case. Maybe. Most do not, in my experience. In addition, it seems that if one is from a "functional" family, they are much more likely to share this kind of experience (but they still don't do it 100% of the time). People will often be interested in it and want to learn more. If you are from a more dysfunctional family, you might be more likely to realize they would put you down and try to shoot holes in your example. They might laugh at you. They might just not talk to you. So, what do you do?

We can extend these ideas to much broader notions such as a clan, a team, a business, a nation. For people who were not lucky enough to grow up in a functional family, the notions of trust and cooperation come hard. And, that's a sad thing. Because your experience of what a bee or a bear or a bank is like will tend to be based on your own experience with very little reliance on the experiences of others. You are one person. There are 7 billion on the planet. So, yes, you can rely on your own experience and dismiss everyone else's. Good luck.

Even a functional family may draw the boundaries around itself so tightly and firmly that anyone "inside" the "circle of trust" is trusted but anyone outside is fair game to take unfair advantage of. At the same time, such a family regards anyone outside as a threat who must "obviously" be out to get their family. People from this type of family do know cooperation and trust, but find it nearly impossible to extend the concept across boundaries of family, culture, or nation. They are happy to hear about their brother's experiences with banks and bees but they are not much interested in the experiences of their distant cousins from half way around the world.

Everyone must decide for themselves how much to rely on their own experiences and how much to rely on close relatives, authority figures, ancient teachings, or the vast collective experience of humanity. Of course, it doesn't have to be an either/or thing. You might "weight" different experiences differently. And, that weighting may reasonably be quite different for different types of situations and strangers. For instance, if your cousin is a smoother talker, vastly handsome, and twenty years younger than you, you might not put much stock in his or her advice about how to "hook up." You might instead put more credence in someone at work who is in a similar situation to yours. You might put very little stock in the experiences from a culture that relies on arranged marriages.

Surprisingly, exactly because that person is from a very different situation and therefore has a quite different take on matters, they may give you very new and creative ways to approach *your* situation. For example, you might find that if you pretend you are already pledged to a partner your parents chose, dating might be less anxiety provoking and more fun. You might actually be more successful. I'm not saying this specific strategy would work or that ideas from other cultures are always better than ones from your own culture. I am just saying that they need not be dismissed out of hand; not because it's "politically correct" to be polite to the customs of other cultures, but because it is in your own selfish interest.

I've already mentioned in the chapter: "Math Class: Who are you?" that people are highly related and inter-connected via genetics, their environmental interchanges, their informational interchanges and through the emotional tone of their interactions. Because people are so highly interconnected, you can find much wisdom in the experiences of others. But there is another, largely underused aspect of this vast inter-relatedness. I call it familial gradient cognition. Or, if you like, "Mom's somewhat like me."

To understand this concept and why it is important, let's first take a medical example. However, this potential type of thinking is not *limited* to medical problems. It basically applies to everything. So, you have a pain in your right hip. What is the cause and how do you fix it? That's your question for the doctor, or more likely, nurse practitioner. They will typically ask questions about your activity, diet, what you've done lately, when the pain comes and goes etc. They may run various tests and decide you have sciatica. This in turn leads to a number of possible treatments. When I had sciatica, I got referred to a sports medicine doctor and got acupuncture. It worked. (Later, I discovered an even better treatment — the books of John Sarno). Anyway, we would call this a success and it seems like a reasonable process. But is it?

The medical professional's knowledge is based on watching other experts, book learning, their own experience, etc. And so they basically engage in this multiplication of experience. The modern doctor's observations are based on literally many millions of cases; far more than he or she could possibly observe first hand. But what potentially useful information was completely omitted from the process described above? Hint: the title of this chapter.

Throughout this whole process, no-one asked me whether anyone in my family; e.g., my mom, dad, or brother had had these symptoms. No one asked whether they had had any kind of treatment, and if so, what had worked and not worked for them. Now, my brother, mom and dad are especially closely related but so are my four children and my grandparents, aunts, uncles, nieces, nephews and grandchildren. And, in the most usual cases, it isn't merely that we share even slightly more genes than we do with all of humanity. We are also likely to share many aspects of diet, routines, climate, history, family stories and values. These too can play a part in promoting health. For example, did people in your family believe in "toughing it out" or were they more of a hypochondriac? The chances are, you will tend to have similar attitudes.

In medicine, would it be better to make decisions based, not just on the data of the one individual under treatment, but on the entire tree of life with more weight given to the data for other individuals based on how closely related they were? Of course, family relations are only one way in which the data of some individuals will be more likely relevant to your case than will others. For instance, people in the same age cohort, people who live in the same area, people who are in similar professions or who work out the same number of hours a week will be, other things being equal, of more relevance than those who are more dissimilar.

As I've already mentioned, modern medicine does take into account the life experiences of many other people. But these other "people" are completely unknown. Studies are collectively based on a hodgepodge of people. Some studies use random sampling, but that is still going to be a random sample limited by geography, age, condition, etc. Other studies will use "stratified sampling" that will report on various groups differently. Some studies are meta-studies of other studies and so on. But how similar or dissimilar these people were to you on a thousand or a million potentially relevant factors is more than 99% lost in the reporting of the data. But that doesn't really matter because the doctor would typically not look at any article in response to your case because he or she will base their judgement on just you and the information they know "in general" which is based on a total mishmash of people.

Imagine instead that every person's medical issues were known, as well as how closely everyone was related to everyone else, not only genetically, but historically, environmentally, etc. And now imagine that diagnostic decisions and treatment options were informed by everyone else's complete medical record, but weighted by how close they were on all these factors. Over time, the factors themselves could become weighted differently under different circumstances and symptoms. It seems clear that this could result in better decision making. Of course, one reason no-one does this today is that keeping track of all that data has historically been too costly. Even if we had access to all the relevant data, people cannot lay out and overlay all these relationships mentally to make a decision (at least not consciously).

A powerful computer program, however, could do this. The result would almost certainly be better decisions. Indeed, this is already being done with respect to known "cancer genes." There are obvious and serious ethical concerns about such an all-knowing system. Misuse might be tempting. Such a system, if it did exist, would have to be cleverly designed to avoid any one power from "taking it over" for its own ends. There would also have to be a way to use all these similarities and prevent the revelation of the identities of the individuals. All of that, however, is grist for another mill. Let's return to the basic idea of the decision making by using multiple matrices of similarity to the existing case rather than relying on rules based on what has been found to be true of people in general.

This may be essentially what the human brain already does. A small town doctor in the last century would see people on multiple occasions; see entire families; and would undoubtedly perceive patterns of similarity that were based on those specific circumstances. The Smith family would all come in with allergies when the cottonwood trees bloomed. And so on. But the small-town doctor would have only seen a limited number of cases even in his or her entire career. Suppose instead, she or he could "see" millions of cases as well as their relationships to each other? Such a doctor might well be able to perform as well as the computer and much better than they could have in the past.

Can it be better done by collecting huge families of data and having a computer do the decision making? Or can it be done better by giving human experts access to much larger data bases of inter-related case studies? Or, is there a hybrid approach that would combine human intuition with machine learning? What are the potential societal and ethical implications and needed safeguards for such approaches?

The medical domain is only one of thousands of domains that could do better decision making this way. For example, one could use a similar approach in diagnosing problems with automobiles, tires, students' learning trigonometry functions, which fertilizers and watering schedules work best for which crops in which soils for what results. You might call this "whole body" decision making. It is a term also reminiscent of the phrase, "Put your whole body into it" (as when cracking a home run into the upper deck, hitting a tennis ace, or hitting a monster drive off the tee in golf).

It is also reminiscent of the following situation. When you accidentally burn your finger, it does not just affect your finger. You jump back with your whole body. There are longer lasting effects in your brain, your stress hormones, your blood pressure. And, various organs and cell types will be involved in healing the burn on your finger. Your body works *as a whole*. But it is not an undifferentiated whole. Your earlobe may not be much involved with healing your finger. Your body is tuned to have communication paths and supply chains where they are needed. It's had over four billion years to work this out.

Of course, the way the body interacts is largely, though not wholly, determined by architecture. Even if your body "decided" that your earlobe should be involved, there is no way for the body to do that. To some extent, it can modify the interactions but only within predefined limits. On the other hand, the brain is much more flexible when it comes relating one thing to another. We can learn virtually any association. But, at least consciously, we are limited to the number of things and experiences we knowingly take into account while making a decision.

What people say might lead you to believe that they very often base decisions on only one similar case. "Sciatica you say? Oh, yeah. My cousin Billy had that. Had an operation to remove a disk and the pain totally vanished. Of course, three months later it was back." It could be the case that there is more sophisticated pattern matching going on than meets the eye. Sadly though, most laboratory experiments reveal that most of the time, under controlled conditions people seem to suffer from a number of reasoning flaws. We could certainly do a better job of teaching people critical thinking rather than having them rely mainly on a few "family stories." And, we might be able to further multiply our thinking ability by giving the right kind of high speed access to thousands or millions of similar cases along with presentations based on how various cases are related.

Indeed, speaking of "family stories" that are common in our culture, I actually think that we have a "hierarchy" of thinking based on a patriarchal family structure. We do experiments and report on a teeny and largely preset sliver of the reality that was the experiment. A person reads about this and remembers a teeny sliver of what was in the paper. When it comes to a specific case, the person may or may not consciously remember that sliver. This is the "rule based" approach and it is probably better than nothing. A more holistic experience-based approach is to allow the current case to "resonate" with a vast amount of experience. (This is somewhat analogous to the approaches to AI based on Rule-Based systems versus Machine Learning). Of course, both methods can be deployed and perhaps there can even be a meaningful dialogue between them. But it may be worth considering taking a more "whole body" approach to complex decision making, whatever the domain.

Perhaps the best decision-making is a family matter.

18 CLAUDE THE RADIO MAN

When I was about seven, I got my first bronzed dinosaur, the Tyrannosaurus Rex. I earned bribe money for being good about getting my butt stabbed by penicillin shots. In any case, I discovered these dinosaurs on the last page of my grandpa's *Natural History Magazine*. The dinosaurs looked really cool! The designers had chosen to make the T-Rex's forearms look more robust than would have been in a perfectly scale model. The T-Rex was great! It was solid and cold and heavy because it was metal. There is something about metal or wood or stone that resonates with me much more deeply than plastic ever could. (Sorry, plastic. I know you are a cool invention and really inexpensive and very malleable and all of that. But, you just don't touch my soul like wood, metal, and stone do.) When I moved the T-Rex, my muscles felt it. Perhaps this is one reason that I still have much of my dinosaur collection 65 years later. (How many of your plastic toys do you still have from 65 years ago?) None is my guess. But they are out there somewhere, along with my own forgotten plastic toys, polluting the world now and for centuries to come.

Bronze, as you have seen many times in your life, does not look worse when it oxidizes, unlike iron does as it rusts. Instead, Bronze turns a beautiful powdery light green with the slightest hint of blue. So, T-Rex looked beautiful as well. You might well think that the next time I had enough cash for one of these statues (1 dollar for the small size and 2 dollars for the large size) I would get another T-Rex. No, I got a Dimetrodon and a

Stegosaurus. Later I got a Trachodon and a Brontosaurus. Anyway, what was fun about this diverse cast of characters is how different they were from each other and the richness with which they interacted. There's no way it would have been as much fun if it were one army of T-Rex's against another. (Poor brontosaurus's tail fell off many times; regrettably, my dad is no longer here to solder it back and anyway, the tail got lost in the last move).

Similarly, a few years later, when I owned toy soldiers, I enjoyed having ones with different properties; that is, mainly different weapons. Liking the variety must have been true for other kids as well because the sets that I bought were always mixed. My favorite soldiers were the hollow lead ones. They were well enough hand-painted that you could see their faces, although not so well painted that you could determine whether they were fighting out of hate, out of fear, loyalty, patriotism, duty, because it was their job, or due to some private demon. I especially liked the bazooka men. I think I had four of them. Of course, this weapon takes a while to reload and there probably aren't a huge number of rounds. There were machine gunners, riflemen (more of them than anyone else), and a couple of officers who were pointing a pistol. There were also a couple of dudes sitting on the ground with a *serious* machine gun tucked between their spread-eagled legs. There were also a couple of hand grenade throwers. Another soldier sported a rifle with a bayonet raised up above his head. This made arranging them for a pitched "battle" all that much more interesting. Although they had very different weapons, all of them had obvious lethal capabilities. All but one.

There was one poor guy with no weapon whatsoever. His job was communications. His only visible "weapon" was a rather large boxy radio set. I suppose in a pinch, he could have whacked someone in the face with it. Even if that didn't kill them, it would surely put a crimp in their dinner plans.

It was difficult for me to decide which one of these soldiers I would "be." I liked the bazooka man a lot. The rifleman looked cool. By the way, there were three versions. One type of rifleman lay on his belly with legs spread and the rifle stabilized by his elbows on the ground. Another type of rifleman sat on the ground and put the rifle across his upright knees for support. The third type, and my favorite, was the proudly standing rifleman. Thinking about it from an adult perspective, he's probably the guy who was voted by his platoon: "most likely to die quickly." But I didn't think about that then. Sometimes, I thought it would be cool to be the officer pointing the pistol. Obviously, in most ways, it wasn't as devastating a weapon as a rifle. Although, in very close quarters, he might outmaneuver a rifleman. But there was one guy that I definitely did not want to be.

You guessed it. I never wanted to be the guy on the radio. Let's call him "Claude." Claude didn't get to actually fight! And, it seemed to me at that point that I could stay alive no matter what obstacles and enemies were thrown at me — if only I were an excellent enough rifleman (or bazooka man, or pistol-wielding officer). On the other hand, it seemed as though "anybody" could do Claude's communications job and would do it equally well. Furthermore, it seemed any enemy could just walk right up and shoot this dude Claude before he could transforms his awkward radio set into a lethal weapon. Of course, Jason Bourne would be able to do it, but I don't think Claude had that kind of training. And, anyway, the first Bourne movie didn't come out until 2002 and this was the early 1950's. Treadstone didn't exist back then. (Or, so I'm told).

These hand-painted lead soldiers were my favorites but I owned three other types. One type were packaged as collections of a dozen extremely detailed beautiful lead soldiers. These soldiers were expensive and, as I quickly discovered, not very durable in real "battles." When you smashed them into each other, the horses tended to break, or what was more typical and worse, not break completely but bend into an uncomfortable and unrealistic position. At that point, I would very carefully ease the broken leg back into position, Angstrom by Angstrom… Snap!! It would break off in my hands. That was worse. I felt as though I had personally snapped that beautiful white horse's leg in half. It always seemed as though I could ease it back into position and I *almost* succeeded each time. Then, SNAP. Suddenly I was holding a three legged horse in one hand and a piece of horse leg in the other. My favorite of these collections were the "Coldstream Guards" with their white and bright red uniforms with splashes of gold. It was sad, I can tell you, to be an eight year-old general and not be able to put your most beautiful soldiers into battle. But, beautiful as they were, they were fragile. I did manage to break a few of the hardier hollow leaden ones as well, but I had to work at it.

Then, there were unpainted plastic soldiers. Packaged in plastic bags; they were molded in a kind of gray-green suggestive of olive drab. Let's call it "off-olive drab" like the olives from that jar of garlic clove filled green olives that you accidentally left at the very back of the fridge for five years. Then, when you finally discovered, it, the olives looked as toxic as rain forest frogs. The plastic soldiers were not a beautiful bright warning color like poison tree frogs. Instead, these soldiers were so drably off-olive that you almost didn't see them. But it wasn't just their uniforms that were off-olive drab. Their entire bodies, including even the little flat plastic stands, their expressionless faces, and their normal-sized (well, normal scaled I should say) hands exuded that same toxicity of colorlessness. Their one giant advantage was that they were far cheaper than the painted leaden ones. And, whereas the fancy ones were fragile and the leaden ones were rugged but breakable, these all-plastic soldiers could not be broken. For some reason, I do know that they can be cut with an ordinary steak knife provided you have enough patience and are smart enough after you're caught the first time "ruining" the steak knives, to make sure the second time you experiment when you're alone. The plastic ones can also be melted with a match. However, melting them had the side-effect of greatly disturbing my parents because of the toxic fumes that permeated our house. (I think we will have to leave for another time the question of why I wanted to know these things). One great thing about these plastic soldiers was that they were to the same scale as the metal ones. So, they could all participate in the same battles without stretching the credibility till it snaps like a rubber band and stings the palm-soul of make-believe.

Ah, but there was as well a fourth type of soldier. These were *insanely* cheap plastic soldiers! A hundred soldiers for a dollar! I ordered two sets so I would have an amazing two hundred soldiers along with the probably 75 I already had. And then they arrived. Yay! Imagine! My army would now rival those of Caesar, Hannibal, Grant, Patton!

My first clue that something was terribly wrong was the size of the shipping box — unbelievably small for 200 soldiers. I opened the boxes and got to the actual soldiers. They looked to be in 2 point font. They were approximately the size of one of the feet of my other soldiers. These soldiers gave a whole new depth of meaning to the expression, "cheap plastic." These soldiers were fabricated out of some material that was like what plastic uses when it isn't about to bring out the good stuff for company. And, "fragile" doesn't quite do justice to the care with which these teeny slats of plastic needed to be handled. Oh, by the way, speaking of "slats," did I mention that they were two dimensional? Did I mention that not only couldn't you discern the motivations of the solider from their face, you couldn't discern whether they even had faces. These soldiers were not of molded plastic; they were basically stamped. In fact, each solider had to be detached from a long plastic rod by twisting.

How could I have possibly known I would waste my two dollars? The picture that the manufacturer used to advertise for the soldiers depicted something very different from their actual product. The picture showed something every bit as detailed and colorful and three dimensional as the hollow leaden soldiers. These same comic books also advertised "sea monkeys." In that picture, there are "families" of little human-looking aquatic monkeys. You can tell what mood they are in and how the various family members interact. Well, I thought this was fantastic! But I didn't totally believe it was possible either so I asked my grandpa whether they were real. He said they were just brine shrimp. I also saw that there was a teeny asterisk in the corner of the picture, half hiding in the seaweed that some of the "sea monkeys" were harvesting for the family meal. Then, in almost unreadably tiny type, the asterisk was explained in a tiny footnote: "visual depiction may not precisely duplicate visual characteristics of crustacean provided" or some equally incomprehensible legalese gibberish that very few 8 year olds are going to comprehend.

Apparently, we live in a society where that's okay. I think part of the reason it's okay is that we live in a very differentiated society. If you think about the single artist, craftsman, or chef, they are much more about substance than puffery. You don't typically expect someone who *makes* something to be dishonest about what it was they created. However, hiring a advertising expert brings into play a different set of factors. The advertising person cannot make a better painting, or chair or soufflé. Their expertise and their "product" is in making people buy the specified product. If they can lie, exaggerate, or mislead and get away with it, so long as sales go up, that is a win for the advertiser. Needless to say, they would never describe what they do as a lie. After all, who would advertise a "lie" as being a "lie"? Then, people might not want to buy one. Advertisers have a whole raft of explanations as to why what they are doing is really in everyone's interest. They've rehearsed it and perfected it and —- since this is what they are expert in — they will probably have you agreeing with them. I'm not sure it *is* just fine and dandy, especially when it's combined with a low quality product such as brine shrimp or "toy soldiers" that are too small to be used or played with as toy soldiers. In these cases, the actual product is nothing like their depiction.

It gets a bit murkier when there are unstated but implied benefits. BMW actually does make a fine car. However, you are not going to be driving it long if you drive it the way it is portrayed on TV commercials. Similarly, a car is not going to stimulate the snappifying head-turner among young people seeking a mate that the advertisers would have you believe. It isn't merely that advertising tends to have us spend money on products and services that aren't really filling our needs, although that is problematic. As a society, we spend a huge amount of money on junk food, cosmetics, and so on; more than we do on truly useful things like medical research. But in addition to that, doesn't false advertising seem to undermine the meaning of truth in *all* human discourse? Or, is it okay for advertisers to lie because advertisers are doing it for money? In other words, is it okay to lie if you are benefiting yourself, because you are undoubtedly benefiting your client as well?

We are becoming more and more connected electronically. This is good news. And this is bad news too. One thing, though is certain. The potential impact of a lie is now tremendous and much greater than it was in the past. In olden times, a lie impacted only the local scene. Now, a lie could literally destroy the world. The balance point of when it's "okay to lie" is different than it was 20,000 years ago — if it ever were okay.

I believe there is a way for people to provide value to each other honestly and still have a thriving economy. In any case, even if we never reach that point and advertisers continue to oversell products, can we at least have the fortitude not to let that attitude toward the truth permeate *every other* aspect of life? A large, complex and highly differentiated society can only exist in an atmosphere of trust. You must trust that the drivers of the other cars on the road are not trying to kill you. You must trust that the food you buy is not poisonous. You must trust that the policeman is there to protect you. If that trust breaks down, there is no longer a society. So intentionally lying in order to make a buck (or a point) is really a push toward utter chaos and anarchy. Obviously, no single push will bring us there, but we must be careful. Why? Because lack of trust is contagious (as is trust). A slight imbalance between trust and mistrust could become a vicious cycle. Information is the reduction of uncertainty, not its multiplication.

A communication network of people becomes more valuable as the number of people in the network increases. A network of, say, 350,000,000 people is much more valuable than 10 relatively homogeneous networks of 35,000,000 each. And, to take this to the extreme, it's much more valuable than 350,000,000 networks of one person each. No matter how smart or strong one person is or how many treasure-troves of weapons they have, they are limited. We need to work together, despite whatever differences exist, to accomplish anything of greatness. That's why it's important that we all keep communicating. That's why it's important that we try to be as truthful as possible. That's why I now think that Claude, the radioman, may be the most skilled and crucial solider of them all.

19 CITIZEN SOLDIERS 1: EARLY ENLISTMENT; NO RETIREMENT

Congratulations! You're in the army now. Well, maybe not exactly in the army and hopefully, you will never have to face combat situations month after month. But make no mistake — regardless of your age, mobility, fitness and so on, you might well find yourself in a "combat situation." Instead of a an AK-47, you might not have any real military weapons at your disposal. You may only have your wits, your experience, and whatever is at hand.

We are all now a new kind of soldier in a new kind of war. This much seems obvious. And although we mostly won't have to face combat or terrorist situations, we will have to be brave and loyal. But we will also have to be smart. It won't be enough to follow orders. Rather than a clear chain of command issuing orders to a loyal army fighting another loyal army, you have already become one of 7 billion game pieces in a complex and giant "game" of war in which the sides are unclear; the objectives are unclear; the boundaries are unclear; and the weapons are anyone's guess. At least one way to think about what to call the "sides" in this war is this: Life versus Death.

In a traditional conflict, whether tribal warfare, Roman conquests, Medieval wars, WWI, WWII, Korea, Vietnam, Iraq, and so on, death is always a possibility. Life and death are always at stake. But what I mean is that in the changing panoply of various sides and nations, there are two large themes in play. One of these is pushing toward those things that foster *life; e.g.,* competition with rules, love, creativity, innovation, science, play, freedom, democracy, listening to all sides, cooperation — these are things that foster life. They do not just foster modern human life. Freedom, for instance, isn't just another word for nothing left to do (Sorry, Janice)*3. Animals caught in a trap will chew their arm off to be free. Diversity isn't some liberal invention of the 20th century. *Diversity is central to the very existence of life.* Life is about experimentation and then seeing what actually works. Letting people play, paint, write, speak as they like — these are extensions of the great human experiment to find out more about our universe and share that information with everyone. These are life-affirming values, not because some political party tries to claim them, but because they are central to sustaining and enhancing life itself.

On the other hand, top-down central control of everything; restricting people's religion, dress, dancing, games, speech, music — these are not characteristics of life. These are characteristics of anti-life. Above all, the forces of Death want to prevent you from gaining knowledge of how life really is. Whether it is making it illegal to paint pictures of birds with naked legs in Afghanistan under the Taliban or defunding public libraries and public education in the USA, the goal is the same: to make sure that your children and your children's children grow up in enslaved ignorance to someone in power. The people who are pro-Death don't say this of

---

3 * Janice Joplin, *Me and Bobby McGee,* 1971.

course. They will make up some crap about how this is in the service of Allah or God or that it's to grow the economy and therefore in everyone's interest. Guess what? It is *not* in everyone's interests. It is not in *your* interests.

The very same techniques that have been honed over the centuries to push your buttons and induce you to buy the brand new horseradish & sea slug ointment that will forever rid you of unsightly elbow wrinkles is also used to make you think you will not only thrive but survive under the new slave order. But you won't. Not only won't the horseradish and sea slug concoction cure your elbow wrinkles. Guess what? Your wrinkled elbow isn't even a problem! You skin is *supposed* to wrinkle at the elbows when you straighten your arm. Of course, once you buy the cream and apply it twice a day as instructed, and you find that nothing in your life has improved, it is embarrassing to admit you've been hoodwinked into spending $29.99 for a month's supply. No one likes to be tricked. But even less do people like to *admit* they've been tricked.

How did you end up in the army? How did I end up in the army? As a kid, I dreamed of being a great warrior, space ranger, or fighter pilot. When did these dreams begin? When did my battles start?

I lived in Firestone Park with my mom, grand-parents and great-grandma till the middle of Kindergarten. The two story white house with green shutters, commanded a strategic view at the corner from which any potential enemy could be spotted. I didn't really play much with other kids during the first half of Kindergarten there in Firestone Park. When I was five, my dad returned from Portugal and Mom, Dad, and I moved to North Firestone Boulevard. That neighborhood sported enough kids my own age to play with. At school, there were no "battles" because teachers separated kids before it got that far. Even so, those would have been more fights than battles. Cowboys and Indians as well as Cops and Robbers served that role. We played and of course I wanted to "win." It's just more fun not to be the dead one. Since we didn't use live ammo or even paintball ammo, who "won" was largely a matter of negotiation. When we first began these games, we tried saying "I got you" but we discovered quickly that others would simply say, "I got you first!" without any regard to who actually got whom first. If one of us were the policeman, we might argue that the good guy should always win. Then, we might argue about that. And so on. Although these games offered some fun, they generally lacked the kind of clear-cut victories we sought.

Later, we learned to play checkers and then chess. You don't exactly get your blood boiling as you might with Cops and Robbers, but at least checkers and chess offered a clear winner. Still later, we learned to play Risk™[4], which I found an enormously fun game. The goal is quite simply to "take over" the world. In case you've never had the pleasure of playing Risk, it's a fairly large game board overlaid onto a vastly simplified map of the world. (Of course, *every* war map is necessarily vastly simplified. Decisions about where to bomb are more

---

[4] TM: https://www.hasbro.com/en-us/product/risk-game: 2C7C6F52-5056-9047-F5DD-EB8AC273BA4C

complicated if you're distracted by the death and destruction of people, animals and property that you really have no beef with and most likely, have never even met).

The Risk™ "armies" consisted of tiny painted wooded cubes. I believe my original set contained "armies" of bright yellow, bright blue, bright red, black, pine green and pink. The map was divided into the Continents. The Australian Continent (which included Australia, New Zealand, and all of Indonesia) consisted of four "countries." Europe had seven "countries;" Africa, 6; South America, 4 and so on. The version I own now has plastic armies which are not nearly so cool as the original wooden ones.

Risk™ was also cool because, although there was a definite element of luck, strategy played a huge part in whether I won or lost. I generally won. I think I liked winning mainly because of this: as I won more and more land and acquired more and more armies, this meant I had more and more choices in where I deployed my armies and where I attacked. Meanwhile, my "enemy" had fewer and fewer armies, territories and fewer choices about what they could do. As a kid, I never really considered that the friends I was beating at this game had less and less choice about what to do as I conquered more territory.

My strategy (hardly original) was to capture Australia and Siam. If you occupied "all" of Australia, you got an extra two armies every turn. Over time, this is a big advantage. If you owned all of Asia, on the other hand, you got seven extra armies every turn. The problem though, with trying to occupy all of Asia was that you could be attacked from many different other countries. On the other hand, to attack Australia you only had one choice. You had to attack from Siam. This meant you had to occupy Siam before you could attack Australia. Conversely, if I could hold on to Siam, I could "protect" my occupation in Australia. And, equally important, I would be preventing anyone else from owning all of Asia. Anyway, during the many years I played Risk, I seldom related it in any way to real war, although it was played, as I said, on this crude multicolored map of the world. Is it possible the obsession with the "Domino Theory" and its application to southeast Asia was based partly on childhood experiences with "Risk"? I don't think so. The timing is wrong. Risk came out in 1957 so people born in 1945 would only be 12 when it came out. Baby Boomers would be old enough to *die* in Vietnam; but not old enough to make any policy decisions. Military generals with enough power to shape US policy would have had to take up playing Risk when they were at least in their thirties.

Risk™ was merely a game after all. The game's objective was clearly stated in the rules. The objective was to take over the world. It never occurred to me that this goal might be something "bad." I understood, even at 12, that the other players also wanted to take over the world for themselves. Someone winning didn't result even in a hiccup in friendships. Angry words were never spoken. However, if someone thought someone else was cheating, then that was an entirely different matter. We had to try to resolve that before moving on. Generally, on the few occasions that that occurred, I think the person accused of cheating said it never happened and we all said something like, "OK, but don't let it happen again." This kind of indicates that we did not totally believe their story. Actually, it isn't quite true that my friends never got angry during play. When we played with two sides, we didn't get angry. Three or four sided Risk™ did result in some angry words. The reason was that when one person began to win (usually me), the remaining players would gang up. But these alliances were only temporary. Once another player became dominant, the alliances would shift to prevent the new dominant person from "winning." Then, the old allies might begin to fight verbally. Managing these fluid relationships was much more difficult than managing how to arrange the armies on the board. It involved another set of skills entirely. Moreover, to "win" at *that* game never struck me as being quite as honest as winning at two-person Risk™ or at checkers or chess. To win at 3-person or 4-person Risk™, you needed to manipulate others into seeing your interests and their interests as being aligned knowing full well that at some point in the future, you would have to attack your ally in order to win the game. I could never really put my heart into this aspect of the game. As a result, I eventually much preferred 2-person play which was an overt and obvious all-out competition from the beginning to end.

My cousin Bob (3 years older and who also became a psychologist) liked multi-person Risk™. He spent a lot of time trying to manipulate me into doing things I didn't really want to do. Perhaps we can delve another time into my credulousness when it came to my cousin. In my own defense, I would remind readers that when you are a little kid, you generally believe that someone three years older knows more than you about how the world works; he is someone to learn from, after all. In fact, not only does the older kid know more, they actually are most likely smarter. Their brains are not just filled with an additional three years of knowledge; their brains are more mature; the wiring is more complete. Anyway, on one particular occasion, we were having a toy soldier fight in a sandbox at his house. His dad, a psychiatrist who ran hospitals for the criminally insane, often moved from city to city and one of our typical summer vacations was to visit him in his new location. At this point, he ran a maximum security psychiatric hospital for the "criminally insane" and lived in nearby Hollidaysburg. He owned a large house with a dog run for Bob's collie, Laddie (who was during that visit, sadly, nearing the end of his life) and the spacious yard included a large, hand-made sandbox. This formed the backdrop for the pitched battles cousin Bob and I set up.

We employed the cool hollow lead soldiers that were hand-painted. Anyway, we had each set up our soldiers and we were about to go through our elaborate process to see who would "win" this battle, when my cousin brought up the idea that he wanted to use a firecracker. I objected that this was unfair and that it might actually blow up some of my soldiers besides giving him overwhelming odds of winning. He countered by saying that it isn't just about winning. More importantly, it's about having a good time. And wouldn't it be cool to have an actual explosion in our battle? Now, as an adult, it occurs to me that I might have asked him to let *me* determine where to place the "dynamite" since it didn't really matter to him who "won." Alas, I didn't think of it at the time and so I relented. He ran inside, got the firecracker and some matches, ran back out, carefully placed the firecracker to do the most damage to my troops (and probably therefore win the "game" that doesn't really count so much as having a good time, let's not forget). He lit the firecracker we sprinted a safe distance away. There was an endless dramatic moment while we awaited the inevitable. After the surprisingly loud CRACK-KOOM we walked back to the sandbox, Bob with a happy grin and me with a more resigned visage. Well, I thought, at least it would be interesting to see the exact pattern of destruction suffered by my troops.

And that pattern was…impossible! In fact, *none* of the considerable damage from the firecracker had been wreaked onto *my* troops. All of the fire-cracker damage slaughtered *his* troops. As this slowly dawned on the two of us, I burst out into laughter. My cousin, however, burst into tears and ran inside. I found that extreme a reaction disturbing in someone so much older and wiser. Anyway, I surveyed the battle scene for awhile. I never did come up with a very good explanation of how this (possibly Karmic?) "smart fire-cracker" actually managed to hit only my cousin's troops, especially since Bob had so carefully positioned it to harm mine, or so we both thought. Soon my thoughts turned back to my cousin. Why had he been so upset? It occurred to me that it really *did* matter to him who "won" our toy solider battle — enough to make him cry, at least when prompted by my chuckle. But besides that, and more importantly, it taught me that he had misrepresented how he actually felt in order to manipulate me into doing something mainly in *his* interest while making it seem as though it was in *my* interest.

They say hunting is the only sport where one side doesn't know they're playing. That's how I felt though. I had been playing a game of toy soldiers with my cousin. We had established norms and rules to decide who "won" a battle. Apparently though, my cousin was also playing another game— a game of psychological manipulation. This was a game that no one told me we were playing. Of course, it you are three years older than another kid and the other kid doesn't even know you are in a game of manipulation, it's pretty easy to manipulate them. But now, Bob had spilled the beans. For him, it wasn't just about winning at toy soldiers or checkers or chess. It was also about winning a psychological game I hadn't even known we were playing. I'd like to say that he *never* succeeded in manipulating me psychologically again. I don't think that's quite true, but at least there were far fewer incidents after that.

And that brings us back to the war that we are all in today. Here. Now. This minute. It is *partly* a war of soldiers and positions and weaponry. On that front, the USA is well positioned. However, it is also a war of diplomacy, communication, and finding common cause with reliable allies. It is also an economic war and a scientific war. Although finding and maintaining superior weapons is not the only benefit from having a healthy economy and a large established scientific community, it is definitely one benefit. If a country develops any type of superior weapon before anyone else can develop it, they have a huge advantage; quite possibly one that cannot be overcome.

What might such a weapon look like? It's hard to say. It could be chemical, biological, or nanotechnological. It could be superior robotics or AI. Or, it could be having a huge advantage in know-how about psychological manipulation, especially if the citizen soldiers don't even know they are playing —- and being played.

If I were in charge of trying to "take over the world" today, even if I had a large arsenal of atomic, biological and chemical weapons, I would still have a giant problem. And that problem would be international cooperation in general and NATO in particular. And the "worst" part of NATO would be its strongest partner, the United States of America. If I use atomic weapons or biological or chemical weapons, yes, I can destroy many countries. But they will destroy me and my country. So, that won't work. But what if, instead, I destroy a country from the inside out? What if I destroy the trust and cooperation of nations in general and of NATO and the USA in particular? If I can accomplish that, I can indeed, end up taking over the world.

Okay, that's easy enough to say. But how on earth can you manipulate a country into destroying itself? If I thought this had not already been figured out by many other people a long time ago, I wouldn't publish it here, but they have so I will. You first look for real problems in that country. Let's take, as a random example, America. There were real problems even in 2016. A small selection in no particular order: gun violence, crime, opioid addiction, unemployment, crumbling infrastructure, soaring medical costs, giant and growing wealth inequality, soaring cost of higher education, insane levels of greed and corruption, a distracted public that wants to "get" everything in two minutes or less, polluted air and water. So, these are real problems that could be used as scaffolding for a full scale attack on our country. These are like the Medieval ladders that allowed the enemy to scale the castle walls. But ladders alone won't do the trick. After all, these are all problems that can be ameliorated with intelligent direction and hard work provided people cooperate. First, they need to cooperate on a way to prioritize issues and pay for solutions. Second, they need to cooperate in the execution of every necessary plan. So, no, scaling ladders alone won't do it. The existing walls are too strong and high.

The second weapon that must be brought to bear is the catapult. And, this catapult is not your grandmother's catapult. It is an "intelligent" catapult. It doesn't just uselessly careen boulders into a mud puddle in the courtyard. No, these flying rocks are guided to the fault lines in the castle walls. Where are the fault lines? What fault lines, you ask? Well, the "fault lines" are the lines drawn in the sand between people when they can be psychologically manipulated into pointing fingers. "It's your fault!" "No, it's your fault!!" Everywhere you can find people divided on an issue, you can aim your catapult to toss a rock there. It doesn't even matter how trivial the issue is! All that matters is that there are at least two sides (two is probably best) and that they fervently disagree. It can be much more entertaining to point fingers and yell at another group of people than to sit down and calmly pick a problem and then go solve it together. Nearly everyone I know personally would experience much better feelings solving problems and building solutions than pointing fingers and screaming. And, yet, the "finding fault" is addicting. It makes you high. It really does. And, like heroin it actually solves precisely the same number of real problems in the real world. Zero. Zip. Nada. Two groups of people can scream at each other for hours, days, months, years, decades. They can throw insults; they can point fingers; they can lob bombs. But not one thing has been accomplished that even begins to counterbalance the damage done in the process. And, meanwhile, there are the opportunity costs of not working together to create something useful, or beautiful, or just awesome!

America has always been something of a delicate balancing act. We celebrate freedom of speech, for example, and this results in hearing some very extreme views. We embrace diversity which supports creativity and resiliency. On the other hand, it also means it may take a little more work or a little more time to understand each other. And so on. But what if someone sought to upset the balance? What if someone's idea of how best to destroy America is to put their fingers ever so slightly on the plates of those scales? And what if the way that they did that was to exaggerate and inflame the various "fault lines" in America and in so doing, greatly weaken the castle walls so that scaling them would be much easier?

That, friends, is why every Citizen Soldier in every country needs to be wary of psychological manipulation.

We need to avoid focusing on finding fault and differences among ourselves and instead focus on finding a soluble problem and then going out and just solving it. Yes, it's great to be brave and loyal. But you've also got to be *smart*. Think about it. Companies spend millions of dollars on commercials to get people to buy their products. Do you think they would do that if advertising were ineffective? Now imagine a country that wants to weaken the US. Do you think they would line up atomic weapons and tanks to shoot us but then fall short of using techniques of psychological manipulation that inflame our hatred and exaggerate our differences? They sure as heck would not be sponsoring radio programs to air uplifting stories of cooperation across our differences! No. It is a war. We are all soldiers. But we must be smart. Think this through.

20 CITIZEN SOLDIERS 2: WHAT KIDS CAN TEACH THEIR PARENTS

Growing up in the semi-developed neighborhoods I did, we never had enough kids of the same age to play football, baseball, or even basketball with full teams. One upside of that was that we learned to modify our play according to how many kids showed up. For example, we often played basketball one on one or two on two. More rarely, we played three on three. One common variant of baseball we called "Three Dollars." One person batted by throwing the ball in the air themselves, then quickly positioning that throwing hand onto the bat in order to hit the ball. The other two, three or four players were "fielders" and if they caught a fly ball, they would receive "$1.00." If they caught it on the first hop, it was $.50 and a deftly caught grounder netted you $.25. In effect, this was just a way to keep score. No money ever actually changed hands. Whoever earned at least three dollars, then got to take the batter's position. In my experience, everyone would rather be the batter than one of the fielders. Anyway, fielders also lost this symbolic money. If you went for a fly ball and dropped it, you lost a dollar. Similarly, you would lose money for bobbling a one-bouncer or grounder. This game seemed to be pretty well known throughout America so I'm sure we didn't invent it.

We did, however, try tweaking the rules. For example, we sometimes played without the penalty clause. You gained but never lost "money." But we decided to go back to the "original" rules. Then, another time, we decided to try it with a different goal, five dollars. After we tried that a few times, we all agreed it took too long to get a turn at bat. So, again, we returned to the original rules. Another slight variant that came up was that not all fly balls were equally difficult. On the one hand, a sharply curving rocket line drive is very difficult to grab! A blooper fly ball is easy; in fact, easier than many grounders. On the other hand, for us at least, a towering fly ball was again quite difficult. So, we experimented with awarding various amounts such as $.75 for an easy blooper but as much as $1.50 for a sharp line drive. It proved that there were too many "boundary cases" to make this a pleasant way to spend an afternoon. None of us really wanted to waste time arguing instead of playing baseball! That was the sort of nonsense that parents engaged in, but we kids were smarter than that.

On the other hand, each of us instinctively knew that we also had to "stick up for ourselves." We could not just acquiesce in the face of injustice. Quite naturally, each of us would tend to see things a bit differently. Let's say I am in the outfield and have $2.00. Now, you, as the batter, hit a looping fly ball/line drive which curves and sinks. I make a nice catch. Yay me. But now I start trotting up to the plate because $2.00 plus $1.50 for a line drive puts me at $3.50 and it's my turn to swing that sweet honey colored bat and knock that little ball for a loop. But you say, "Whoa! Hang on there, John. You only have $2.75!" And I say, (and, please note that there is no baseball going on during this exchange) "No way. That was a line drive! That was a hard one too!" (And, I mean that in the sense that it curved and sank and it was actually quite a hard catch to make.) So, then, you say,

"What? That wasn't hard! I caught a lot of line drives that were harder than that one." (And, what you mean by "hard" is that it was high velocity.) Generally speaking, we resolved these disputes but after 3 or four of them, we made a firm decision to revert to the original rules. In an entire season, under the "normal rules", there might be one questionable call as to whether a ball was caught at the very end of the first bounce or just after the second bounce began. But the categories of fly ball, one bounce, two or more bounces — these withstood the test of time.

There are some interesting balancing acts inherent in the "design" of these rules. I am positive that this game was not invented by a single individual who used a mathematical algorithm to determine the appropriate "values" for the various fielding plays and what the stopping rule was and whether or not to extract penalties. Kids tried out various things and found out what "worked." The rules and the consequences were simple enough (and easily reversible) Our small group of kids determined what worked for us. For example, if we made the changeover goal dollar amount too little; e.g., $1.50, the turnover was too fast. Too much time is spent running in to take the bat one minute and then running back out again later to field. No-one got to "warm up" in their position enough to play their best. To the batter, if felt like a real win to be able to hit the ball and, in a way control the game. Because, any half-way decent batter, if they are hitting from their own toss can easily direct the ball to left, center or right field and can also determine whether they are hitting a likely fly ball, one bouncer or grounder. So, for my own selfish reasons, I wanted the game to go as long as possible with me as batter. So, it made sense to hit more often to those players who had low amounts or less able fielders so as to "even up" the game. This also made it more exciting for the fielders because it made the game "closer" for them. An unwritten code however, also kept this from getting out of hand. For instance, if I began by hitting two hard line drives to the left fielder, and they made great catches, it wasn't really okay to simply ignore them and never hit to them again until everyone else had caught up.

Many potential rule changes never even came up in conversation. For example, no-one ever said, "Hey, let's count $.98 for a fly ball, $.56 for a one-hopper and $.33 for a grounder." We wanted to spend the summer (or at least much of it) honing our baseball skills, not our arithmetic skills. And, while we soon discovered that we did not want to spend our time arguing about the boundary between a line drive and a fly ball, we knew without even trying that we definitely didn't want to spend our time practicing mental arithmetic. And, we further instinctively knew that people would make errors of addition as well as memory. It was pretty easy for the batters and other fielders to keep track of what three people had when left fielder had $2.50, center fielder only had $1.50 and right fielder had $2.75. No way did anyone want to remember current scores such as, $2.29, $2.85 and $2.95. Then, the left fielder misses a grounder and you subtract $.33 to get to $1.96. No. Not happening.

We wanted rules. We never simply had one person bat as long as they felt like it. And, we definitely didn't want to argue after every single strike of the ball whether it was time for someone else to bat and if so, who that might be.

So, the rules were really helpful! They were simple. They were fair. And they minimized arguments. We experimented with rule changes but in every case, decided to go back to the original rules. And, there were many potential rules that we never even discussed because they would be silly, at least for my neighbors and friends.

In addition to all the formal rules, unwritten and mostly unspoken codes of conduct also framed our play. If someone "had to" bring their much younger sibling along, for example, we didn't hit a line drive at them as hard as we could. We knew that that wasn't "fair" even though it was within the rules. Fielders tended to "know" how far each batter could hit a fly ball and positioned themselves accordingly. Someone could have pretended not to be able to hit farther than 100 feet; keep drawing the fielders in and then bang it over their heads so they had no chance of getting a valuable fly ball. But no-one did that. It was understood that you hit the ball as far as you could. Fielders also positioned themselves far enough away from each other so that running into each other's implicit "territory" proved rare. "Calling for" a ball occurred but not very often. We never had to say aloud, as best I can recall, that you were not allowed to "interfere" with each other's catches. Implicitly, even though the fielders were competing with each other to take the next turn at bat, the fielders were modeled after a real baseball game and so, in effect, the fielders were all on the "same team" just as they would be in a real outfield or infield.

A number of interesting phenomena occurred around this and similar games but the one I want to focus on now is that we experimented with the rules; we changed the rules; and if we didn't like the new results or process, we changed the rules back to the way they were. And I find this relevant today because I find that many of my colleagues, classmates and friends seem to want to "return" to a set of rules for conditions that no longer exist. I totally get that and in many ways can relate. It seems doable because many of us have had similar experiences both in sports and in other arenas where we try out a new way of doing things and then decide the old way is better. In my experience, this worked and with very little argument. I don't recall spending time in my childhood screaming about whether a $5.00 limit or a $3.00 limit was better for the game. We started with a $3.00 limit, tried a $5.00 limit and then we all agreed $3.00 was better. There may well be places where the particular group of kids decided on $2.50 or $5.00 limits. But is there any group of kids who beat each other up over this? Is there even a group of kids who preferred the $2.50 limit who refused to play with the $5.00 kids? I don't really know, but in my observations of kids whether my role was parental, grandparental; whether familiar or professional; whether at camps I attended or ones where I was a counselor; whether in a psychiatric hospital or a school setting, I have never seen it. That doesn't mean it doesn't exist, but it can't be *that* common.

In our small group of neighborhood kids, we were able to "roll back" rules pretty easily and smoothly. It *seems* as though we should be able to do this on a larger scale, but I just don't think that is possible. It may or may not be desirable for various specific instances, but I don't think for many situations, it is even possible; or, at the very least, the costs are far higher than we would be willing to pay.

Consider some examples from nutrition. When I was growing up, my parents and grandparents inculcated in me that I was supposed to eat "good" meals which included meat or fish every single day. At some point during my adult life, there came to be concern about cholesterol in the diet. The theory was that cholesterol contributed to heart disease and that you should avoid eating foods like beef, eggs, and shrimp which contained a relatively large amount of cholesterol. Now, we believe that refined sugar and artificial sweeteners are both far worse food sources than are beef, eggs and shrimp. In fact, most of the cholesterol in your blood is made by your own liver and only a little comes from your diet. But eating a lot of sugar causes you to store rather than burn body fat and also makes your cells eventually "immune" to the regulatory effects of insulin.

People have always had differing tastes when it comes to food. Some people have completely ignored every bit of nutritional advice that's ever been put out there. They eat what they feel like eating. Others are willing to try any new hyper-health fad that comes out. Most people are somewhere in between. But because there have always been people eating beef, eggs, and shrimp, repopulating these into your diet is pretty easy. It is one case where we really can roll back guidelines.

But imagine instead of having a change in nutritional *guidelines,* we all subscribed to a religion which had made eating any birds or bird products strictly taboo for the last thousand years. And, let's imagine that was true world-wide. Now, a new religious revelation reveals that actually, birds are quite good to eat and so are eggs. Now what? There are no chicken farms. There are no boxes made to carry eggs. There are no companies whose business is to provide eggs. There are no egg inspectors. There are no regulations about breeding chickens or gathering eggs. Indeed, it is a lost art. There are no recipes that use eggs or chicken. People don't realize that some people are quite allergic to eggs. People don't realize that eggs "spoil" if they are kept warm too long. The point is, that unlike my little coterie of kids deciding to go back to $3.00 instead of $5.00 (which was easy), the adjustment of adding chicken and eggs back into our diets would be a mammoth deal. There would be many mistakes along the way. A few people would even die of food poisoning. Still, my guess is that it would prove possible. The benefits would eventually outweigh the costs. Even so, there would be a lot of disruption. People who sell soy products, for instance, might well claim that the religious revelation was bogus and that eggs and chicken should still be banned. Even people who are persuaded that it is not a sin to eat eggs might still think they are pretty gross because they have been brought up that way. Family stories have been passed down over generations. Perhaps Aunt Sally once tried an egg when she was little and that's why she grew up cross-eyed. (This isn't the real reason, but it might be the reason in a family story).

The point is that we can "change" this way of doing things, but it will be much more disruptive than changing the rules of our ersatz baseball game. Other changes are even more difficult to pull off. Partly this is because in a complex interconnected society like ours, any change away from the status quo will hit some people harder than others. Just like our "soy producer" in the egg example, whoever is "hurt" by a reversion to something older will not like it and will struggle socially, politically, and legally to keep things they way they are now. They will not want to go back to how things were (or, for that matter, into a future which is different either).

Most of our ways of doing things are now highly interconnected and global. For example, the computer I am writing on at this moment is far, far, more powerful than all the computing power worldwide that existed when I was ten. While I know something about how to use this computer, I do not know the details of how the hardware works, the operating system, the application that I am using, and so on. This computer was produced and delivered by means of an extremely complex global network and supply chain. The materials came from somewhere on the planet and probably no-one knows exactly where every part of the raw material even came from. The talent that conceived of the computer, designed it and built it was again from all over the world. Apple does business in at least 125 countries throughout the world. Other major companies are similar. The situation is nothing like having 125 separate companies in 125 different countries. These companies are all linked by reporting relationships, training programs, supply chains, communication links, personnel exchanges, and so on. If, for whatever reason, Apple decided to become 125 different independent companies — one for each country, they would, I believe, fail very quickly. It would be nearly as difficult (and as sensible) as if you decided that you no longer wished to be an integrated human person but instead you now wished your arms, your legs, your head and your trunk to operate as six separate entities.

We are now *vastly* interconnected. Certainly, WWI and WWII were deadly global conflicts. Not only were these wars costly in money and human life, but they were horrendously disruptive as well. Families were broken apart, infrastructure was destroyed, supply chains were interrupted. New hatreds flared. But even as lethal and costly as these wars were, WWIII would be much worse even if no atomic, biological or chemical weapons were used. Why? Because nearly every country in the world is now tightly interconnected with every other country. Maybe that was a great idea. Maybe it was a horrible idea. Maybe it's a good idea in general, but we should have been much more thoughtful and deliberate about the details of how we inter-relate. Regardless of how wise or unwise globalization has been, we cannot simply "change the rules" back to the way they were 100 years ago. The field of play has been fundamentally altered.

If we attempt to destroy globalization, and have each country "fend for itself," it will be incredibly expensive both in dollars and in human lives lost. The genie of globalization, however much you hate it or love it, will not squeeze back into that magic lamp. If we attempt to go back 100 years, we will actually go back about 2000 years. Consider this computer I am using. I worked in the computing field for 50 years. And, I would be completely helpless to try to make anything like this computer from scratch. But the computer is far from the only example. Could I fix my car? Some things I could but the engine diagnostics now require a computer hook up. Could I fix my TV? Not much. My dad was an electrical engineer. The most common cause of problems with a TV in my youth was that a vacuum tube stopped operating properly. When the TV was "on the blink" we would take one or more tubes out of the TV and take them to a testing machine at the grocery, drug store, or hardware store and see which tube needed to be replaced and then buy that replacement, go back home, put in the new tube and *bingo* the TV worked again! Can I do that today? No. Can you? I doubt it. But it isn't simply electronics and automotive industries that are global and complex. It is nearly ever aspect of life: financial, medical, informational, entertainment, sports, and so on. What about your local softball team? You know all those people personally just as I knew the folks I played $3.00 with. But where were your spikes made? How about your softballs? Bats? Mitts? The last bat I bought — a beautiful, heavy aluminum bat — came sheathed in plastic. I think that was unneeded pollution, but there it was. Where was that plastic made? Where did the bat come from? Where was the metal mined? Where was it fashioned?

On the whole, I personally think the highly interconnected world we live in is more fun and interesting. In a typical week, I literally eat food inspired by Mexican, Japanese, Indian, and Thai recipes. In many cases, it is prepared by people originally from those countries. Books, plants for gardens, music, movies, games — these things are made worldwide and distributed worldwide. To me, it makes life much more interesting. I fully realize that globalization isn't everyone's "cup of tea." If you don't like globalization as much as I do, you can certainly stick to cuisine, authors, music, dress from your own native land. You're missing out, but it's your call. But no matter how you try, you cannot "disentangle" yourself completely from the larger world. No politician is going to manage it either.

Our inter-connectedness is a two-edged sword that often wreaks havoc as well as providing cheaper goods. Little bits of plastic micro-trash that come from the United States pollute oceans everywhere. Air pollution that originates in Asia comes across the Pacific to sicken people in North America. If the Japanese kill too many whales, it affects the ecosystem world-wide. Pollutants that come from Belgium may kill bees in Argentina. A plague that begins in Thailand may kill people in New Jersey or Sweden. We cannot simply wish this interconnectedness away. Today's "Citizen Soldier" needs to be smart as well as brave and loyal. You are not standing in a long line dressed in a red uniform facing a long line of soldiers dressed in blue (who are your enemy). You are going about your own business. But you must understand that how you treat people from every other country whether you are visiting a country or they are visiting your country — how you treat them will impact people globally. If you treat people badly it will impact you and your neighbors badly in the long run. We really have to think globally even while we act locally. I think it's the "right" thing to do. It's a little hard to imagine a serious world religion or world philosophy that justifies trying to get as much as possible for you or your tight-knit group of friends at everyone else's expense. But even if you somehow convince yourself that it's morally "okay" to be a complete isolationist, reality will not let you do it.

You can take your turn at bat. But you also have to take a turn fielding. Kids who take their first turn at bat and then "go home" as soon as they have to go out in the field do not get called upon to play a second or third time. You might most enjoy being a bazooka shooter. But you are going to have to spend a fair amount of your time being "Claude the Radioman" as well, because with seven billion people on the planet, more coordination than ever is needed. It won't work to have everyone be a "hunter-gatherer" any more. It won't work for everyone to "do their own thing." It won't work to roll back the rules of the last 100 years and have every country do their own thing either. We cannot smoothly "undo" history. We cannot jam the genie of globalization back into the bottle. I have a much better chance of fitting into the pants of my first wedding suit (waist 29") and I'm a long way from that.

I mentioned that in my neighborhood, we typically did not have full teams. One day, however, while we were playing American football (five on five) in a vacant field two blocks down from my house, an older kid approached us explaining that he wanted "his team" to play "our team." We didn't actually have a "team" at all. We would get together and chose captains who would then take turns picking kids for their (very temporary) "team" for that particular game. We had a football. That was pretty much the extent of our "equipment" though someone did occasionally bring a kicking tee. The vacant lot did not have any goal posts so there were no field goals. We generally played a variant of American football, wherein the defenders were not allowed to cross the line of scrimmage and tackle the quarterback until they had counted "One Chimpanzee, Two Chimpanzee, Three Chimpanzee, Four Chimpanzee, Five Chimpanzee" — and then, they could rush in and tackle the quarterback. In the five on five variant, the center was generally a blocker while the other three ran down the field and tried to "get open" so that the quarterback could hit them with a pass. Occasionally, a quarterback would try a run. If they could "fake" a pass and get the rusher (usually only one person) to jump up off the ground, the quarterback could generally sprint past them and gain a reasonable number of yards before the other defenders realized it was a run. (In case you aren't familiar with American football, once the quarterback goes beyond the point where the ball was hiked from, they are no longer allowed to throw a forward pass).

In any case, although five on five football was fun, it also seemed to us that it would be even more fun to play eleven on eleven like "real" American football. So, we agreed to come back the next day after school and face "his team." Weather cooperated and we showed up the next day after school and so did the other team. In uniform. We didn't have uniforms. But not only were they all wearing the same colors. These kids had helmets, shoulder pads, thigh pads, elbow pads and shin pads! They were *armored!* But we weren't! Every time their center hiked the ball to the quarterback, a bunch of us would try to rush in to get the quarterback. No "one-chimpanzee", "two-chimpanzee" business now. We were playing real football. And getting real bruises.

I can tell you that it hurt an unnatural amount to run into these other guys but we held our ground. It did seem unfair to us but they never wavered or offered to take off their pads or helmets. The first few times were not so bad, but once your body is already bruised, then it does hurt to run into someone with full body armor. I suppose it sometimes seemed equally unfair to Medieval peasants without armor who were attacked by armored knights. Hardly a "fair fight" as we would say. Nor does it seem a very "fair fight" for a little kid walking on some distant jungle path to suddenly have their leg blown off from a land mine. And, I suppose some would judge it an unfair fight for a village of unarmed farmers to have a rocket or drone smash their village to pieces along with many of the men, women, children and livestock. Just guessing, but that's my sense of it.

This older kid who arranged our game did not actually play, as I recall, but served not only as coach for his team but also as the one and only referee for the game. That didn't seem particularly fair either, but he was actually pretty impartial. As it began to get dark though and we were still tied, he did make something of an unfair interference call, at least in my opinion. Anyway, I think they won by only one touchdown. We did pretty well against these armored kids from another part of town. But we were a sore lot the next day. None of us suffered any major injury such as a broken bone though we were all pretty black and blue from the battering. None of us were very eager to have a rematch though. We talked briefly about the possibility of getting our own uniforms but we were financially way short of that. Even if we had actually collected all the pretend money we talked about in "$3.00" we couldn't afford that kind of equipment.

Does it matter whether a game — or a war — is a "fair" fight? Or, does it only matter who "wins"? In sports, we generally have a lot of rules and regulations to ensure fair play. We would consider it a gross misconduct of justice to have one pro team denied equipment! Some readers may be old enough to recall the controversy over using fiberglass poles in the Olympics.

I think it may matter more than many think as to whether a fight is a fair one. A fair loss leads most people to acceptance and adaptation; in many cases, it can serve as motivation to do better. But when people think a fight is unfair, resentment will often linger and eventually result in another fight. Chances are that this time, the party who feels they have been treated unfairly will no longer care about having a "fair fight" and do anything they can to win. Anything. So, it serves us well to think long and hard about winning an unfair fight. What will happen next? It seems to me that when we win an unfair fight, there are many negative consequences that almost always outweigh the benefits of the win.

First of all, whoever loses the unfair fight will resent you. Second, people not involved at all in the unfair fight and who don't even care about the outcome, will care about the process and the vast majority will dislike whoever behaves unfairly. Third, it makes it more likely that other people will be unfair in their own transactions.

In the days of childhood sports, we sometimes disagreed about what was fair. *But we never disagreed about whether it was okay not to even try to be fair.* We all assumed we were supposed to be "fair." You must understand, this was unsupervised child's play. We did not play baseball with parents around coaching, umping, and spectating. Of course, we had disagreements and sometimes we lost our tempers. On rare occasions, someone might walk off in a huff. But, there really weren't that many huffs to go around back then, so it was rare. And, whoever did walk off in a huff was back the next day ready to play $3.00 again. Their huff dissolved in the cool night breeze. When they went to their closet the next day, no wearable huff remained. There may have been a few tattered huff-shreds in the bottom of the closet, but not even enough to wear as a bathing suit, let alone a three piece suit of huff; complete with huff vest, huff pants, and a huff coat. I don't think any of us even owned a huff tie.

I think part of the reason our disagreements faded so quickly was that they were face to face. We never sent e-mail. And, we certainly never hired a lawyer to "represent" us. For some reason, when one person "represents" another, they feel it is more "okay" to do unfair things than the person themself might feel comfortable with. We kids simply discovered that it was a lot more fun to play baseball, in any of the variants, wearing a shirt, sneakers and jeans. A huff suit was simply too confining and easily torn. Kids *all* seem to know this instinctively, but as they grow up, they may begin to fill their closet with huffs and wear them on many occasions.

Imagine a world in which adults all donated their huff suits to a recycling center. In that imagined world, adults talked, solved problems, had some fun, and when they disagreed, tried to do what was fair for everyone. It sounds kind of crazy, I know. But we live in a world of miracles, don't we? And, that world is embedded in a universe of miracles. Very slowly we are coming to understand more of it. Our understanding of this amazing universe grows and some of that understanding even sheds light on how our bodies and brains work as well as the fundamental characteristics of the universe. Maybe somewhere in this vast universe of miracles, there is a way to experiment with the rules of the game until we find a way that works for everyone who wants to play. Perhaps we could pay $.25 when someone can restate what you said to your satisfaction. If someone can think of another example of the same principle, they get $.50. And, if someone has a brand new sharable insight on the topic, they get $1.00. First one to $3.00 gets to direct the dialogue for awhile. Come dressed for serious play. No huff allowed.

21 CITIZEN SOLDIERS 3: GALOSHES IN THE GUTTERS.

One of the joys of my childhood was to be lucky enough to be walking home from school after the rain had abated but the storm gutters sloshed to overflowing. The earth smelled clean and the sky sang that pure clear blue note. Part of our wading game was to get the water level as high as possible on our boot tops but not to pour over-brim and soak our feet. This danger provided one source of excitement; also, the water's music thrilled our ears; the water rushed and gushed; pushing against our legs with a rather considerable force. All of our gang had seen movies where people were helplessly rushed away by river currents, sometimes to be flung over waterfalls and shredded on the rocks below. If you would have asked any one of us in your all serious adult "show me how smart you are" voice whether we thought we would be swept out to sea or over a waterfall, we would have answered, "Of course not!" (Yet, secretly, it felt like a real possibility).

Here's the odd thing. Looking back on it, I actually think this is a great strategy for learning. There's a problem with trying to "practice" something like swimming or floating in a raging river. You're much more likely to die in practice that you would in real life! For Navy Seals, of course, the equation changes, and such practice may be worthwhile. But I contend that for kids, doing something completely safe, but a tiny bit like something actually life-threatening or otherwise critical might be quite a good thing if and when that life-threatening situation actually occurred. In the first place, it would help keep the kid from panicking. I'm not saying it would be a perfect inoculation, but it could help. Second, it could teach the kid a little bit about the situation. Yeah, in the case of wading in the gutters, far less force would be involved than in a life-threatening situation, but the kid would still be learning something of the way water works by wading in it and watching it flow in the gutter and seeing what floats and what doesn't and how things tend to get "stuck" in certain places.

Imagine two kids of identical strength and temperament, one of whom had played in raging gutters a score or more times and one who had never done so. Now they fall into a raging river where there is lethal danger. One of them survives. Well, my money is on the kid who waded in the gutters. Every time.

There are many other childhood activities I engaged in that have echoes of such life and death situations as hunting, tracking, avoiding predators, and even war. Most sports involve acts of throwing, catching, hitting, kicking, or knocking each other down. Think of kid's games such as "Red Rover Red Rover" or "Hide and Seek" or "Freeze Tag" or "Mother May I" — each has skills that could help a child survive in a disaster or accident, or, sad to say, war. These days, many kids instead sharpen another set of skills by playing video games. These skills too could come in handy in another class of disasters. It's hard to know which is more valuable because of the uncertainty for our future. Probably learning a bit of both would be good. Personally, I like video games but I'm very happy for having waded gushing gutters.

One of those glorious afternoon wades home, however became a horror show. At that time, I was probably around ten years old. My two best friends were 9 (Bobby) and 11 (Home). The nine year old Bobby had a younger brother, Billy. We were all walking home in sight of each other, but Homer and I were about a half block ahead, I think on Austin Street. We heard a scream and looked back to see three teen-aged boys holding Billy by the ankles threatening apparently to drown him. Bobby was trying to get his brother loose, but they swatted him away like a fly.

Suddenly, our pleasure had turned to pain. Our friend Bobby was up there trying to get his brother loose. What should we do? I looked at Homer and he looked at me trying to discern a clue to the right action. I am not still not sure what the best response would have been. Four pre-teens against three teenagers would be an extremely one-sided contest. Boys don't get any real strength until their hormones kick in and that wouldn't happen to us for another few years. At that age, bigger boys do not just have more strength and range, they are also cleverer and know more. Any way, maybe we should have charged back up Austin street with fists windmilling, but what we actually did was run home to get some adults involved. (Inexplicably our cell phones were non-existent because of the linear time assumptions we all accept as truth). I am glad to report that Billy did not drown and no-one was seriously hurt. But it did ruin our enjoyment of gutter-walking. First, we wondered if those giant teenagers would reappear another time. Second, it always made us wonder whether running to inform all three mothers had been the best tack. It certainly wasn't the bravest and we definitely had an urge to help our friend and damn the consequences. But then again, it might have enraged the biggies even more and all four of us might have been actually injured. I, at least, also felt guilty because it was a ubiquitous rule among us kids that you don't involve parents if humanly possible not to.

One of the most despised type of kid any of us ever ran into was that kid who would go running to their parents at the slightest or most trivial affront. I'm not talking about someone who gets slammed against a wall and breaks a rib and tells their parents (though even then, it's a close call). I'm talking about someone who forgets to collect their two-hundred dollars when they went around GO in MONOPOLY and then goes running to mommy. "Mommy! Mommy! They won't give me my $200. They're cheating!" Mommy, who, of course, knows absolutely *nothing* about what just happened, comes in and says, "Now, boys. You'll have to play fair. Give Timmy his money or you'll all have to go home."

The third and final unpleasantness, of course, is that it made me feel inadequate. If I had only been older, stronger, faster, smarter, bigger, then I could have charged them with such a fury they would have backed off and never darkened our gushing gutter play again! At that point in my life, I don't think a thought such as, "If only I had a weapon like a knife or gun, then, I could have handled them" ever crossed my mind. But I can totally understand why it might well cross the mind of many youngsters today. It might indeed do more than cross their mind; it may well inhabit their mind and become an obsession. If I have the right weapon I will be adequate to defend those I care about.

Other folks may take a different tack and go full bore into body building. Some folks might think: "I will be so physically strong, I will be able to defend those I care about." Still others might mainly focus on trying to acquire sufficient resources to defend those they care about. In our society, if you have more "things," and more money, it can make the difference between life and death; for example, when it comes to expensive health care or even being able to afford housing away from major toxic pollution sites. "I will be so rich, I will be able to take care of and defend those I care about."

My own reaction has been somewhat a mixture, but my major obsession has been to find ways that humanity can get out of its own way and solve its problems cooperatively rather than blowing each other to smithereens. "If I can be wise enough and persuasive enough, maybe I can help defend those I care about."

When it comes to "defending" there are many possible paths and all of them have value under various circumstances.

These days, it seems that there are enemies of many sorts. Computers may have brought many good things but they have also enabled an unending assault on our senses easier than ever. I seldom even answer my own phone any more because I get so many spam calls. E-mail is serviceable but barely for a similar reason despite various spam filters. Social media is filled with click bait,

"Do this one simple trick with a honey crisp apple and a fax machine and never die!" "These pictures of celebrity X with celebrity Y will make your hair turn white and your shoes into thousand-league boots." And so it goes. This is an annoying enemy but only deadly in the long run.

A much more short term threat is imminent terrorism. Everyone in America agrees that having our citizens murdered is not a great thing. However, people's ideas about what to do about it are quite varied and probably correlated with the approaches they take toward making sure they can defend those they care about. I am not sure what the right combination of approaches is in the short term; probably all the strategies outlined above are appropriate.

I also know that over-generalizing about people being "bad people" based on their skin color, toe length, religion, country of origin, age, gender identity or sexual orientation is counter-productive. I understand it's based on the same generous motive: trying to defend those you care about. This is a motive I share. People are too malleable and flexible to be rewarded or punished on the basis of where they are from or who they are. It is reasonable to reward and punish people for their *actions* if those actions have a significant impact on others.

Sometimes one person's acts because that act is vastly important to that person and their liberty but that act only has a passing and minor effect on someone else. For example, perhaps you prefer people to walk down the street at a particular pace. People who slowly hobble down the street are a temporary minor annoyance to you. But what is the alternative for them? Never to go outside and walk? By the same token, you may not like joggers zipping in and out of crowded sidewalks. They make you nervous. Or, maybe they make you feel guilty because you're not jogging. Maybe your particular sect of your particular religion doesn't believe in jogging. Whatever the reason, for you to try to outlaw jogging entirely because it's a temporary annoyance to *you* is absurdly egocentric. On the other hand, if you can show that jogging is dangerous and has serious consequences for many people, then outlawing jogging needs to be taken seriously. But it's still rather silly to *hate* joggers because you find them annoying.

In any case, singling out any one group will not, on balance, help you defend the people you care about. Why? Because such actions will alienate an ever growing circle of people. Some of those people will end up with weapons as good as yours, a body as strong as yours, resources as rich as yours, learning as great as yours. Such efforts to "weed out" terrorism actually plays out more like the New England fishermen who fought the starfish that preyed on their shellfish by tearing the starfish into pieces — each of which produced a new starfish! That's not to say terrorists are starfish, but unless you are very careful in how terrorism is dealt with, you will definitely recruit more terrorists.

Wouldn't you react that way? I mean, just suppose you are a small business owner. You've been pro-US your whole life. You live in Syria and you are a Muslim. Now, people invade your neighborhood and destroy your business. Some of your close family are killed. Now, you are welcomed to America with open arms. Do you really think you're likely to become a terrorist and help destroy the country that welcomed you? Not impossible, I grant, but not bloody likely.

Now, contrast this with a situation where the same businessman suffering the same civil war begs to come to America. He explains that he is a Muslim but is a big fan of America. He wants to be a productive citizen. He has a grand-daughter he's never seen already living in the US. But no. He cannot come in because he is a Muslim. He tries as best he can to defend those he cares about. But he and his entire family are wiped out, except for his grand-daughter in America and one of his sons who survives though his leg has been shattered. The son curses his father for the pro-American stance, that, at least in the son's mind, led to the death of his family. Does he join ISIS? Damned right he does. It has nothing to do with religion. He doesn't become more religious or more Muslim in his heart when the takes to the path of violence. It is a desire to seek revenge. He cannot defend those he really cares about because they are all dead. But he can make those who caused the death pay dearly.

Part of the difficulty of course, is that everyone is an individual and reacts differently. The same survivor above might have gone a different way. He might have decided Bashar al-Assad was at fault and dedicated his life to destroying *him*. He might even have decided Putin was at fault; without his support, al-Assad would have fallen long ago. It doesn't seem quite fair to go around destroying the lives of people because they *might* be justifiably angry.

Let's say my neighbor's dog attacks and severely bites and kills one of my cats. Should I be now deported before I become violent? Should I be jailed because I might exhibit the rather bizarre (but somewhat understandable) behavior of killing my neighbor? Would it matter if I told you I was a Christian? A Jew? A Muslim? An atheist? Maybe I should mention being 1/8 or 1/16 Native American so no doubt there is savage blood in there too, right? What if I'm a Jew but married to a Muslim? What if I studied the Koran and the Bible but actually think of myself as a Zen Buddhist?

A society that begins to punish people for what they *are* (which they can't help) or for what they *believe* (which can never be proven or measured in detail) rather than for what people actually *do* is a society well on its way to destruction by its own hand[5]. This is especially true because the actual physical threat to the citizens of the USA and many other countries, while real, is way down on the list of things to worry about. However, that could change. And one of the main ways we can make it a hundred or a thousand times worse is to start punishing people for some broad religious category that can be attached to them. This will certainly grow the number of terrorists and terrorist sympathizers.

---

[5] Dumbledore: "It is our choices, Harry, that show what we truly are far more than our abilities." - *Harry Potter and the Chamber of Secrets,* (1998) J.K. Rowling.

But there is another way to aid the terrorists and that is by over-dramatizing and focusing on terrorist events. The worst terror attack I know about is 9/11 where more than 3000 people from around the world died here in America. At the time, there were over 300,000,000 Americans most of whom were "terrorized" by the event and its aftermath, at least to some degree. I'd much rather be "terrorized" than be one of the 3000 dead, but in total, there were five orders of magnitude more people "terrorized" than killed. Meanwhile ten to twenty times that many world wide were also more or less terrorized. The actual death of a person happens once, but a terrorist event can be relived and reported and talked about a thousand times. Naturally, this is not to say that professionals should not investigate attacks or try to develop increased security techniques that actually work.

If we put stopping terrorism at the *top* of our agenda, and are willing to do literally *anything* to defend against terrorism including subverting the Constitution, then we have multiplied the effectiveness of the terrorists far beyond what they themselves are capable of. If we stop working together to find and solve problems and instead start pointing fingers at each other as the source of all our troubles — game over.

Game. Set. Match.

The carefully laid firecracker laid there with the intention of destroying one side has actually destroyed the other side.

Instead, we need to mostly forget about the "big kids" that hang out on Austin Street. We can't jail them just for being big kids. But we have to develop a number of solutions to make sure they will never pull that trick with Billy again.

Meanwhile, we should not let glancing over our shoulder, a necessary caution, keep us from sloshing down those gurgling gutters in our galoshes.

So, here we all are, somewhere on earth. Each of us is unique; a product of our evolutionary, cultural, and personal histories. I am convinced that the vast majority of us are trying to do our best regardless of country, party, religion, race, or background. And, before launching into a discussion of anything else, it is worth at least a few moments to reflect on the fact that we have changed our world tremendously even in the space of my personal lifetime. I was born in 1945, the year the atomic bomb first devastated human lives. Since Hiroshima and Nagasaki, seventy three more years have passed without an atomic war. Of course, there is no guarantee that there won't ever be one but we have survived decades when we might have wreaked this kind of heartless havoc on each other. And, we haven't.

Another thing that impresses me is that we regularly communicate and cooperate with people across the world. Countries share ideas, products, services, and people. True enough, war persists. Yet, generally, people today enjoy the lowest death rate by violence at any time in our history. (Of course, if you or a loved one is a casualty, there is little comfort in knowing that "in general" people aren't killed as much by violence as they used to be). But the general decrease is fairly remarkable when you consider a few vital accompanying changes. First, we have far deadlier weapons than ever before. Don't get me wrong, if you smash someone's skull with a large rock they are every bit as "dead" as if you drop a bomb on them or poison them. But, today we can kill a great many people at a very great distance. And whereas the strongest and healthiest and best-trained knights may have had a much better chance of survival than weaker or less able cousins, today it does not matter how well-trained you are or how much you can bench press. You will not survive in close proximity to an all-out attack whether by atomic weapons, chemical weapons, or biological ones. Second, we have far more people on earth than we ever have before. We evolved to be hunter-gatherers. We lived in small tribes. Now, we have 7 billion people on this planet.

Imagine that there is only one large pie and four people all must satiate their appetites from that one pie. They might discuss things a bit. Maybe one person would claim to be famished while another does not really care that much for pie but would like to taste it. I would not foresee much trouble with four people. Would you?

Now, imagine that instead of four people, you had four hundred people and they only had one pie to stem their hunger. Wouldn't you expect a much louder level of argument if not actual fighting to break out? Now, imagine that instead of four hundred people, there were 40,000 people and the only thing to eat was that one pie? Of course, there is a good chance for violence. However, it might also be possible that they would realize one pie split 40,000 ways is not much improvement over nothing. Why fight? It might be better to do a lottery and have the winner lay claim to the whole pie. If they liked, they could share with their friends and family. This may not be great, but it is probably still better than having everyone fight for the pie. Or, people might decide that they will have a contest based on what they value most.

If they value physical strength more than any other human attribute, they might have a shot put contest or a wrestling match. The winner of the contest would get the whole pie and would be free to wolf it down themselves or to share as they saw fit.

Suppose that everyone agrees to a wrestling contest and as the semi-finalists enter the ring, many are shocked at the discrepancy between the apparent physical abilities of the finalists. Odysseus, let's call him, sports legs like tree trunks, arms thick with banded muscles. Despite his giant proportions, he walks like a lion displaying a quick, easy grace. By contrast, Cassius, say, appears a bit on the thin side. His gait impresses the crowd as someone who might stumble or fall frequently. How can they both be one match away from becoming champion?

Here's how. Cassius isn't using his *strength* at all. He's using *poison.* As in ancient Greece, contestants in our mythical world wear gloves. Cassius, for each of his previous matches, has put a nearly undetectable ointment on the outside of his gloves. He touches his opponent, and they begin to get weary; they nearly fall asleep. But before they are so clearly drugged that foul play would be obvious, Cassius headlocks his disabled and wobbly opponent. The crowd mainly attributes his success to having, despite appearances, a terrifically effective headlock. Why do they do this? They are prone to give Cassius the benefit of the doubt. They do not assume or presume that when someone is successful despite a rather obvious lack of relevant talent, that every one of his previous matches was due to nastiness and breaking the rules.

Now at last, it has become clear. Cassius has succeeded only by some foul means even though the precise nature of that means is not yet clear. The crowd grows restless. Cassius was supposed to embody what the crowd agreed was the most important, best defining characteristic of their hero: physical strength. Instead, Cassius does embody a trait — treachery — a willingness to say one thing and do another; a willingness to break any and all rules in order to win the entire pie for himself.

It would be wrong to say that treachery is never a good trait and it would be equally incorrect to say that immense physical strength is always a good thing. To take one example, what if you appear to agree to be a spy for invading space aliens but meanwhile tip off the humans and thus save humanity from certain annihilation? It seems to me that an ability to be that "treacherous" would be good. On the other side, imagine two people; one a champion body-builder and the other on the week side. Each of them becomes frustrated trying to level a door. The weaker one pounds the side of his fist on the door twice to vent frustration then goes back to leveling the door. The stronger one, however, whams the door with his fist hard enough to break the door and embed his hand into the splintered wood. He becomes trapped there and bleeds out through his shredded brachial artery.

However…

It needs to be noted that in the hypothetical case of the wresting contest, everyone had already agreed that they wanted their champion to be the one with the most physical strength, not the one most willing and able to be treacherous. Odysseus played the agreed-upon game and stood poised to win. Cassius on the other hand, did not argue with the crowd and try to convince them that treachery trumps strength and therefore it should be a treachery contest. No. Cassius pretended to agree to play the game of "who is stronger than whom" but what he really played was the treachery game all along. In a way, this is not all that surprising because that is the game he is best at. Cassius isn't so deluded as to think that he is better at actual wrestling than Odysseus.

The thing that I find surprising about this scenario is that people didn't catch on much sooner that Cassius was not winning his matches through ability but through treachery. As I said, I believe one reason for this is simply that most people are willing to give others the benefit of the doubt. Second, while many might have admired Odysseus, others may have been secretly resentful. They realized that they could never be as agile, as strong, as skilled as Odysseus. On the other hand, when they looked at Cassius, they might think, "Hey. Here's a regular guy like me. If he can win the pie, it'll be almost as good as if I get the pie! Anyway, he promised to distribute ten of these pies to everyone if he wins, so maybe, just maybe, I won't think about other possible ways he could have ousted bigger, stronger, faster opponents."

Of course, as more and more people come to recognize the fundamental treachery of Cassius, the ones who knew of it and backed him anyway become ever more vested in their original choice and therefore will not admit that they knew all along. They keep on cheering for Cassius: "Look at those biceps! No wonder he beat all those others! Killer headlock! Go Cassius!" Others in the crowd look at the biceps of Cassius and what they see is pretty damned ordinary arms; if anything, a bit on the puny side. There is nothing they see that says: "Look out! Killer headlock!"

So, here we find a divided crowd. Those people who believe *ability* is most important believe basically this: "This is insane. Has the rest of the crowd gone blind? How can they speak of the ability of Cassius as being the cause of his success. It's poison and we will prove it. And people guilty of treachery will be punished."

The Cassiusts, on the other hand, believe: "…that treachery wins the day and, in fact, that it is a kind of wily intelligence. The human race didn't get where it is because of strength. We aren't anywhere near the strongest. But we may well be the wiliest. We set traps for other animals. We learn their habits and hunt them down. We bait hooks for fish. We domesticate other animals for our purpose. All of it hinges on a kind of treachery. As they say, hunting is the only sporting event where only one side knows it's playing. Anyway, there's always been treachery in politics, hasn't there? It's smart to win any way you can."

Yes, I agree it is smart to win any way you can, but only under the following two conditions:

1. *What counts as you winning is only what happens to the protoplasm inside your skin.* That attitude is off by *many* orders of magnitude. As discussed in an earlier chapter, most of "you" is outside the boundaries of your own skin. Most of what is in the interest of Cassius is not within the boundaries of his own skin but also in everyone else in the entire crowd and therefore how his actions impact them, is on the whole, hugely more important than the impact on himself, even from the standpoint of self-interest.

2. *What counts as winning ignores the long-term and systemic effects of treachery.* One note does not make a symphony. The pie splitting contests are not a one-time deal. People play over and over and over again. If you use treachery, you encourage treachery in others. Yes, if everyone else is trusting, you will gain a lot in the very short term. But in the long term, you will be punished right back. And your descendants will live in world that is much more ruled by treachery than ability. It's actually a long-term lose for *everyone,* including those who are "best" at treachery and that is true regardless of whether you are "found out."

Meanwhile, what is even more important is what is *not* happening to the extent it could. While people argue about how the pie should be split and who should get to decide, the actual business of living is *not* getting done. Diseases are *not* being cured. People are *not* getting the education to the extent they could. Better international cooperation and mutual respect is *not* being accomplished. Better roads are *not* being built. Crumbling bridges are *not* being repaired. Scientific discoveries are *not* expanding our knowledge of the universe. Affordable healthcare and wellness are *not* improving.

What this amounts to in the hypothetical example is that people are *not* creating more pies. They are too busy fighting about who should be awarded the pie. This is the other reason why treachery is not a reasonable value for a society to hold dear, let alone primary. Treachery leads to treachery. And, although it is true that those in power can do a lot of dictating, no matter how heavy-handed a reign of terror becomes, it is always subject to overthrow and revolution. And, during such a struggle, we are essentially fighting over who gets how much of the pie and — oh, by the way — killing each other in the process. Neither tyranny nor revolution is conducive to making all that many pies. That's why rewarding treachery and cheating is antithetical to the whole idea of any society whatsoever; or to any form of cooperation.

There is room for legitimate debate about *which* qualities are most important for who it is who gets to decide how to split the pie (e.g., empathy vs. intelligence; creativity vs. experience). If that same person also gets to decide how much energy we put into making which additional pies, this adds another set of important qualifications. If splitting pies is the champion's only job, being fair-minded, open-minded, generous, would seem to be good qualities. If the decider also had a large role in determining how many and what kinds of new pies to create, then, being vastly knowledgeable and intelligent would be vital; being able to communicate across disciplines and interests in order to make difficult tradeoffs would be important. In the best case scenario, this person would take in good ideas from all angles and help produce even better ones on output.

The only scenario that justifies wanting a treacherous leader would be to imagine that we live in a completely treacherous world internationally and in that sense, there is a "fixed pie" model of the world economy. What France gains, I necessarily lose and vice versa. This is, by the way, an insanely incorrect model of the world. It is far more cooperative than competitive. Of course, this is not to say that countries do not sometimes compete for Olympic venues or airline contracts. But this is overwhelmingly accomplished without treachery by staying within agreed upon rules of the game. People don't always agree with every specific rule; they may try to change them, but for now, everyone's agreed to play by them.

Yes, under the incorrect scenario of a treacherous world, having a treacherous leader would make some sense, but *only* provided treacherousness was "maxed out" because otherwise it is still in someone's best interest *not* to be treacherous. Of course, the other critical proviso is that we would have to completely trust that the "Treacherous King" would be treacherous only to *other countries* but honest and above-board with the citizens of his own country. A Medieval king or queen may have been able to pull off an illusion of doing this. I submit it's impossible today except for a few dictatorships where news from the outside world is heavily censored. When people have access to the internet and social media, for example, you cannot say one thing to one nation or group or crowd and a completely different thing to a different crowd or nation or reporter. So, it seems completely paradoxical to have a leader who is maximally "treacherous" to be of *any* long-term value. You couldn't trust him on a long-term basis and neither could any other nation. Once trust is completely gone, it takes a long time to win it back. As a strategy, treachery seems a really out-dated one. If you really love treachery, I can see why you would want to cut back on education, quash any dissenting views and so on. Without that, you couldn't get it to work against your own citizens more than once or twice. If you prevent people from ever finding out, it will take longer. It won't take forever. But it will take awhile. And meanwhile, treachery metastasizes throughout the land. I like to think the immune system of the crowd is sufficiently strong to treat such an ugly and pernicious tumor successfully or isolating it from the rest of the body. These are the best ways. I am hopeful that humanity survives the 21st Century and that the earth will be greener, fairer, and less violent in 2100 than it is today.

Hope, though important, is not enough.

It is our choices, readers, that show who we truly are.

ABOUT THE AUTHOR

John Charles Thomas was born in May of 1945 - the year that atomic weapons and digital computers both began to play a significant role in human life. He spent the first three and half years in Akron, Ohio which was then the "Rubber Capital of the World." He moved to Portugal where his dad managed a factory and returned to Akron in 1950 where he attended public school in Firestone Park and Ellet. He has always enjoyed writing and worked numerous jobs during college such as camp counselor, grader for math papers, projectionist, child care worker, research assistant, science teacher, and recreation director. He attended graduate school in Experimental Psychology at the University of Michigan where he earned a Ph.D. degree in 1971. His first post-graduate job was managing a research project on the "Psychology of Aging" at Harvard Med School. In 1973, he joined IBM Research where he did research on human computer interaction and speech synthesis for about a dozen years until leaving IBM to become Executive Director of the Artificial Intelligence Lab at NYNEX Science and Technology. He rejoined IBM Research in 1998 where he spent more than a dozen years working in human computer interaction, knowledge management, cognitive computing and tools for high performance computing. He worked on IBM strategies for bringing computing to the "Next Billions", "Smarter Planet", and "Cognitive Computing." During this time, he also became a fellow at the Institute for Rational Emotive Therapy and became a licensed psychologist in New York State. He has been very active in the Associate for Computing Machinery's Special Interest Group in Computer-Human Interaction (SIGCHI) and was awarded the 2018 SIGCHI Lifetime Service Award. He retired from IBM in 2013 and moved with his wife, Dr. Wendy A. Kellogg, to the San Diego area where he writes, consults, and plays tennis. He has four children and twelve grandchildren.